Bob Flowerdew's
AutobyBobraphy

volume 1
a foreign county...
early days, 1953-1965

"The past is a foreign country: they do things differently there" wrote L.P. Hartley in his 1953 novel "The Go-Between", also set in Norfolk

CONTENTS

a foreign country   **page 4**

a family history   **page 90**
Notable Flowerdews
Tendency to write
The Kett Rebellion
Strange death of Amy Robsart / Anne Dudley
Taking the roof off the Abbey
Ancient Planters, founders of the USA
My personal family tree
Fictional Flowerdews

Bob's other books   **page 101**

a foreign country

A cuckoo called incessantly throughout a cold windy East Anglian spring day, the last of April, only ceasing at dusk as I emerged into this beguiling world, into a rural backwater lingering a half century behind in time as I was to discover. More 1903 than 1953, almost as if someone had pressed a pause button.
Of course I've not remembered the day though my mother Pam oft repeated the tale 'blaming' the cuckoo for bringing her the wrong baby. She'd survived difficult labour in truly Medieval conditions in a farm cottage to bring forth a boy, when she'd anticipated, even expected and wished for a girl. She'd so wanted a daughter, had so convinced herself I was to be that girl that my readied baby clothes were pink. Still this is my story not hers.
My earliest memories are of being cold and or damp, in the dim, dank or dark too much of the time. I was born into a home lacking improvement in comfort since glazed windows had been introduced. Such would now be considered 'quaint' being one room through, barely habitable, with head banging beamed ceiling, uneven brick floor and a stable door at the side. Back then such unimproved houses were common enough, un-modernised, un-insulated, damp, and exceedingly draughty with scant heat coming from open fires. About as snug as taking shelter in a barn.
At first, I'm told, my parents managed without any services whatsoever, no electric, no phone, no mains water thus no WC, bathroom nor shower. A house perishing cold all winter through, though at least pleasantly cool on hot summer days. Home was as we'd now say totally 'off grid'. Though

my parents were not proto-hippies, they were just caught in a post war low wage rural economy. Thus although we had no services neither did most of our neighbours, things have always advanced more slowly in the country. Electricity as it only needed wires had reached most villages, mains water supplied many if not most though far fewer were connected to mains sewage. Telephones, again needing only wires, were reaching out, then multiplying or rather dividing as party lines became private. 'Town' gas had never and has still never been available in many country villages let alone to outlying folk. The Postal service was universal though and would deliver letters, parcels, and Telegrams though these last were expensive and unwelcome as likely bringing bad news. Generally houses were being improved though slowly with both a shortage of manpower and materials even when funds were available.

Thus in such rural areas the world immediately about remained much as it had been at the end of the Victorian era. Two World wars had been economically hard on the whole country, then as towns and cities recovered and raced ahead progress only slowly penetrated rural hinterlands.

Looking back my childhood was a rural idyll, well it was in summer, and closer to the fictional dream than would be possible for most children now, or even back then. But other than during the warmer months throughout much of year it was cold and simply not very comfortable.

Until I was eight Mother cooked in a lean-to of corrugated iron sheet on the back of the house lit after dark by the glare of paraffin Tilley lamps. Brighter than most electric lights these emitted strong hissing noises, and were pressurised so needed pumping up regularly. Candles and the more common paraffin lamps (with wicks), were less noisy, less bright, though just as smelly. These were our lights in the house and outdoors if we had to venture out. An ex military battery hand torch was father's and forbidden, too valuable on a farm to risk losing. For the coldest weather we lit a Valor paraffin oil heater which would slowly make the room less cold, this could also boil a kettle or saucepan on top. It also gave off an odd smell, along with huge amounts of water vapour making everything even damper and the windows would run, in deep winter becoming ice which built up in weird thick patterns.

The fireplace set in the chimney in the middle of the north wall in our 'living' room was too small for burning logs of wood and coal was burnt on the open grate. Conveniently we lived opposite the local coal merchant so never ran out even in the worst freezes. An open grate gives off a lot of heat, most of which rushes straight up the chimney, with only radiant heat close to, so your front is hot and your back cold. They do not warm the room as all the air is being sucked up the chimney so you need be very close to the fire for the heat. Most country homes had no central heating anyway and still burnt similar coal fires, the more prestigious having one in every room including bedrooms. Also most kitchen stoves and ranges for cooking, and the water boilers for washing, 'Coppers', were often still coal or coke (coke was gas-extracted-coal, lighter and cleaner) powered. Indeed where a house was important enough and had pre-war central heating that, and the greenhouse, boiler would be likely be coal powered. Firewood was needed to start and sometimes augmented coal but was seldom in great supply probably as this was before chainsaws were widely introduced and had ripped our woodlands bare. Thus gathering any quantity of firewood was hard work. And also because although coal is smellier you burn less volume of coal compared to wood and on a smaller grate getting more heat given off than from wood.

Through most of the darker months of the year we were sent to our beds just for warmth. Old fashioned beds these stood higher off the ground than modern divans, in the 'warmer' air not the coldest layer near the floor. For bedding we had linen sheets with a serious number of thick wool blankets, then 'eiderdowns' and finally crocheted wool patchworks. Plus our hot water bottles. Though rubber ones had been invented we still made do with clunky old stoneware pottery ones, rock hard comfort even when covered in a crocheted cover. If you know not the scant joy from cuddling one of these be forever grateful.

Little plastic was yet about so much pottery persisted, as with those hard old hot water bottles, and the now 'jokey' chamber 'pots' under our beds. These were necessary for night use as our 'toilet' was in, an unlit of course, brick shed way down the garden path. And we would have to pass through our parents' bedroom which had the stairs down, before we could make any expedition outside.

This outdoor toilet was brutally cold in winter though nostalgically rustic in the warmer months, with bluish white-washed walls and worn wooden seat over a bucket, all under a canopy of honeysuckle over an old apple tree. With torn newspaper squares hanging from string for both economy and in preference to that totally ineffectual scratchy greaseproof paper sold so inappropriately for the purpose (I remember a brand called Bronco, what an inappropriate name.) After finishing the paperwork we sprinkled soil or sawdust over the bucket's contents which was transferred when brimming to holes made under fruit trees in our orchard.

Looming over this khasi and supporting the honeysuckle, both presumably being well fertilised with centuries of accidental overspill, was a Lord/Lady Henniker, a local apple, large, oval, green with red stripes. Intended for cooking these kept well and were eaten raw throughout half the year despite being as hard as a Sugar beet and not quite as sweet.

Our garden was large though much was barely kempt orchard. Father, unlike most farmers, did garden and had a rudimentary vegetable bed four square out the back, with almost everywhere else down to rough grass. He only grew a few vegetables, the basic necessities of onions, carrots, beetroot, cabbages, peas and potatoes. We also had a beautiful purple flowered Clematis clinging on the end of our house, a few old bush roses beside the path going around the vegetable beds, and, such modernity, a clump of Pampas grass. I still have a fondness for this brute which often cut my fingers but gave me wonderful sticks topped with plumes to wave and throw about.

Beyond the partly filled in orchard ditch was the 'wood'. (In this ditch were wild strawberries, not the 'modern' Alpines but the truly wild runner'ing sort with small spherical very aromatic berries.) The wood was an ancient moated enclosure where we let our hens run. In my childhood the moat had half dried out leaving wide gullies with hanging ropes of Old Man's Beard / wild Clematis and Ivy, which we were not supposed to swing on... A few strong oaks at the edge predominated but much of this 'wood' was Elderberry, a weedy shrub full of insects in flower and then full with birds when in fruit, and Stinging nettles, a plant which I seem to have encountered near every day of my life but especially when in short trousers.

Our homestead nestled within fields on a little used road opposite an even less used lane that accessed little but more fields. A short distance along the road lay our village centre with pub, shop, post office and garage. Quite a metropolis for a country village though bear in mind this was the fifties so these were bleak, unwelcoming and sparsely stocked with the little then available.

Most buildings had long become run down from repeated wartime privations, had never recovered from the first let alone the second great war. Indeed rationing only ceased the year I was born, special issues for cake making were apparently given out for the Coronation celebrations that summer. There was a general feeling of shabbiness, little had been repainted or repaired and much really was very much as it had been for centuries past. Our ancient church stood in a curve of the main road close to the village well still in use when I was tiny. Opposite was our village hall, a long wooden shed of more recent design not dissimilar to commercial hen houses on nearby farms.

Out in the sticks
This village of Yaxley lies south of the river Waveney on the old Roman road running northwards from Ipswich to Norwich. The road crosses the Waveney from Suffolk to Norfolk just north at Scole (known locally as Osmandiston, a name now forgotten) and just beyond that Dickleburgh where my mother's family lived and where I loved to be most.

Scole had an old stone bridge, now long gone, this scenic relic was replaced by a concrete one when I was small, which in turn has been replaced again. The old road has now become a riverside park and picnic site. This areas been re-wilded, nestled amongst ancient soaring grey willows enlivened with dragonflies in summer, many birds even Kingfishers to be spotted. It is only a small park but much like how far more of the area was when that bridge was built in stone. Apparently also similar in unforeseen ways with lurid tales of 'dogging parties' in the car park on summer nights, goings on perhaps not so unfamiliar in times past either.

A bit of a misnomer the Waveney valley is seldom discernible as such. Arising on the edge of Breckland a few miles to the West and feeding into the Norfolk Broads on the East this river itself is often little more than a slightly wider than most, shallow muddy ditch, more seeping than flowing between watery meadows. These are picturesque with lush grass and grazing oxen elegantly framed by edges of Sallow and towering Grey willow. Most fields remained small as the pressure for huge prairie farms had only just begun. Likewise the roads were and are mostly narrow, winding, some with passing places. Many furnished with high verges topped with even higher hedges to shield off the bitter winds.

Little of this scenery had altered since the days before the Romans had come and gone. In fact they drove their straight roads through the existing field pattern which had arisen for centuries before they invaded. A patchwork of small fields, many hedges and small copses, splattered with clay lump farmhouses and humble cottages painted pink (originally a sacrifice's blood was mixed with whitewash for 'good luck' later replaced by chicken's).

True, there had been changes, the village was bisected crossways by a disused railway that had once run past on its way down to Eye. This had needed a bridge for the main road over the rails, one of the highest points around with views into the distance. (You do not get many views in these parishes, as the land is so flat unless you're elevated all one can see is the next hedge or row of trees. Thus one can cycle along a road apparently entering a forest, it just never condenses remaining as scattered trees in copses and thick hedges simply continue on seemingly forever.) This redundant bridge built by the Victorians had many small stalactites hanging down inside. I knew it's age from the metal plate and this was one of those discoveries that made me doubt accepted 'facts'. Viz. the time it took to make stalactites in caves. If they had formed here in just a century...

On the far side of the village lay the concrete outline of a deserted airfield. The Yanks had come and gone in a twinkle, leaving an immense number of huge acreages of concrete, a twang to the local accent, a sprinkling of offspring, and little else other than immense and still emerging quantities of ammunition strewn over all the surrounding fields. (Quite understandably any remaining live ammo was frantically jettisoned when your plane was coming in on fire...)

My father, Richard, kept accumulated finds in a venerable shepherd's wagon long decomposing in the corner of our orchard. In this were all sorts of other curious things: tools of all sorts and unrecognisable devices, half emptied bottles and tins of no longer recommended treatments, wagon parts, horse tackle and war time posters. Most enticing of all to young boys were these stacked boxes and crates full of mostly live rounds of aircraft cannon shells he'd picked up, easily enough to make a seriously massive explosion.

Later when a little older we would sneak in and steal these for their cordite which we insanely liberated to make illicit fireworks. There were also slow burning ropes stored there, each strung every few inches with explosive cartridges, to be hung as bird scarers. A firecracker nay a banger beyond compare, but we knew these were valuable and effectively numbered so could not take any from full runs only the odd old remnant. Whereas the discarded ammo seemed fair game, though so unwittingly risky to play with. Well not totally unknown, one poster showed the different colour coding for the rounds: armour piercing, incendiary, explosive, we studiously avoided the latter.

Another foolish danger was clambering over the stack of glass carboys of battery acid and transformer oil amongst the decaying trucks and motors behind the village garage. This backed onto our hen run situated in our old moated wood. The moat on that side had become a stagnant pool with oily surface and floating discarded light bulbs. What joy to pop one with a well aimed pebble. The old cars left rusting were a great play ground but we had to be quiet or we got spotted and told off. In a shed was an even more appealing relic, a wartime monkey-bike motorcycle dustily visible through the window, oh how we longed to get our hands on that!

Across the busy 'main' road was a village shop deemed out of bounds as this road was considered too dangerous for us children, and even some older folk, to cross. An early brush with death was riding my tricycle along the pavement, one wheel going over the edge tipped me into the road under a passing truck, which most fortunately had seen the mishap about to happen and was already braking so I missed serious injury by a whisker. The traffic on this road seemed unable to cope with S bends and accidents happened so often neither I nor most other kids were allowed to play in any roadside gardens.

The other village shop was also the Post Office, uninviting, dim, drab and dreary, don't forget there was little on sale then compared to a decade later. Both shops were somewhat irrelevant anyway as seldom did any of us village kids have any money. Though when we did we would rush to get halfpenny chews and with sufficient cash a biscuit confection called Wagon Wheels (called as these were so generously proportioned, progressively becoming smaller over the years – by now should be renamed supermarket trolley wheels.)

Sweets indeed had only just become available again, remember rationing had just ceased when I was born and the grim parsimony of wartime hung on. Little 'modern fare' was available and especially out in the sticks thus our meals were almost entirely traditional, bland but wholesome fresh farmhouse cooking. Bread, eggs and home grown vegetables, home made cakes, jams and chutneys and whatever meat had been too badly shot up to sell.

Most families kept chickens, ours had their run in that old moated wood beyond the orchard. Long overgrown so full of places they could hide their nests, we spent hours crawling through the undergrowth searching these out. We sold eggs, which are most valuable when scarce in winter and especially after the New Year as folk then bought eggs to hatch at home. The reason was eggs hatched before Easter give hens that start to lay the next mid-winter when their eggs would be most valuable again. Later in the year when the demand for 'sitting / hatching eggs' passed we could eat more. and gloriously, more cakes were made. Some eggs we stored for cooking 'out of season' immersing these in large jars of Water-glass (Sodium silicate) solution. As with many of our neighbouring farmers we ate what we could not sell so meat was as often rabbit or game. Wild bunnies were strongly flavoured but we also kept New Zealand Whites in cages and their flesh was much more delicate, rather like chicken. Their food was surplus garden vegetables plus wherever we went we would pull Hogweed (a Heracleum but not the giant poisonous one) to take back for them, this has small bristles which irritate and burn the skin, but such trifling pains were casually ignored.

For a while to help my family get by a relative lent us their old house cow, a Dexter. This is a small breed for home use and although small should still have given considerable milk. Was a shame, and in a way fortunately, it gave little milk, especially as it turned out to be riddled with several diseases. Anyway milking and looking after a cow took too much time as we had little use for as much milk as it did give, butter was a lot of work with such small batches so much milk just went to the pigs, which loved it. Oddly cheese had not been made locally for as long as anyone could remember, perhaps because it seemed Suffolk cheese had long been reckoned amongst the worst in all the kingdom.

Chores were plenty on a small mixed farm with so many animals to look after and I and later my younger brother Martin, were expected to do many little tasks and errands. With no hindrance from Health & Safety we delivered feed to birds and kine, collected eggs, checked watering bowls, cleared out the ashes, stoked and lit fires, peeled vegetables, cooked simple dishes plucked and even butchered, ran non stop errands and of course fetched and carried especially the lunch out to the men in the fields particularly urgent when the harvest was on.

I liked cooking chores as these had me sitting in the lean to kitchen, a relatively warm place. Indeed I found cooking a real pleasure (especially as like any child I would sneak morsels) and by the time I was ten or eleven could manage most basics including baking pastry and cakes and was able to prepare whole meals unsupervised.

My mother was a fair cook though her mother Nan was much more proficient having been a cook at a couple of 'great' houses including Blickling. She would tell tales of the profligate meals she had once worked on. But that was before the First World War when things had been so different. Two long wars, the depression and rationing especially the shortages of meats, fats and sugar all of which still remained scarce had reduced most English kitchens to the most basic ingredients. Still we did what we could, not always successfully, I sadly remember Pineapple jam made almost entirely from Sugar beet with a dollop of a most unconvincing pineapple flavour, that was indeed poor stuff. Likewise chutneys were stretching the term solely to utilise some surplus. One of the worst was a runner bean, banana (flavour I believe!) and walnut chutney whose jars kept returning to the table till the stringy stodge inside darkened and dried enough until eventually deemed fit only for the chickens.

Cakes were made when eggs were available and bulked out with whatever was handy, grated carrot is traditional and can near double the weight of a cake also making it moister and without losing sweetness. Here again the ubiquitous East Anglian delicacy of Sugar beet made an appearance and cakes were often extended, well dominated, with this as it was also saving sugar.

One other local product I remember with little nostalgia was Sugar beet wine, made by the older boys by a method passed down from some optimist. This tasted like muddy cider but was easily made from purloined sugar beet so was drunk as legitimate stuff could not be had. You cut the top off, made a hole in the centre, put back the bits chopped up with some baker's yeast and stood it to ferment with the top sat back in place to keep the flies out. A few weeks later, well as soon as possible, you drained the 'wine' out. Rumour was if we added raisins we thought this would make it 'brandy', -if we'd had any raisins, these were too tasty and sweet anyway, so would never have got there uneaten.

Certainly homemade cakes were welcome fare however as with most meals there just never seemed enough. Mother's clever question stolen from another mother was "would you like some more as if you won't there will be just enough left over for tomorrow…" Anyway we never cooked too much as leftovers could not be kept long. Few people then had a household refrigerator, anything such as dairy products that needed keeping cool were kept outdoors in a shaded lean-to housed in a perforated Zinc cupboard that kept both flies and rodents at bay. (However milk was delivered daily and came in glass bottles, the knowing folk had the milkman place these in upright earthenware pipes covered with a tile to keep them cool. Later these pipes proved efficacious for stopping the Blue-tits from stealing the cream as these birds learned to pierce the foil caps.)

My first remembered conversation was walking beside my mother with our golden Labrador Sally when she explained that with a little brother coming we would have to get rid of Sally. I was, and still am, heart-broken. I loved that dog so much as she had 'adopted' me and was my constant companion, and warmth, when small. My parents never showed physical affection, to us, nor each other, no hugs, no sitting on laps nor cuddles. It was my father behind this, he'd had a strict Victorian upbringing with a governess till the age of twelve, that and then a harsh school and the Army meant physical contact was abhorrent. No pats on the back or rides, he never ever even shook my hand till his very last days (and that was but the once) and was jealous of any sign of emotion or love by our mother for us. Indeed my brother and I called one uncle, my Godfather, "Big Strong Uncle John" because he would lift us up in the air and swing us onto his shoulders when he visited.

Despite asking on many occasions the true reason for Sally's departure this always remained steadfastly unanswered. I now believe Sally had to go not because we were too poor to feed her, back then rabbits and pigeons were too easily had, but I reckon because I showed too much affection for her and this had irked father. I queried whether she'd been sick and they'd not wanted to upset me, however they said not. Regardless of my protestations at the time Sally was driven off in the back of the farm Land-Rover never to be seen again, while I was fobbed off with my new baby brother. Scarcely a move well calculated to ensure sibling harmony... To be fair, my father had experienced traumatic upbringing, a governess had been needed as his mother Amy had been spoilt and a 'naughty' girl. She'd run off with her sister's fiancée, only to then drop him. She'd then married my grandfather, already an old man (he died before I was born), and then had an affair with 'Uncle Harry', scandalous in a village, and worse, he a divorcee with a history of wife beating. (And back then to get a divorce really did mean serious beating!) All her life she remained a 'flapper' and 'foolish' or 'silly' in so many ways. She married and was then dominated by Uncle Harry, who obviously disliked us kids giving us short shrift when we visited their new bungalow just north of Norwich. (Coincidentally this was built next to the meadows where Black Beauty eponymous horse of the book had grazed, this adding to some of my early confusion betwixt the literary world and reality.)

Although a fair all done-by-rote cook Amy's nervous habits would have her prick the potatoes so often to check if they were done she never got to serve them any other way than mash. Other vegetables fared likewise and seldom reached the plate intact. Mind you she could turn out wonderful pastry, her treacle tart was heavenly (lemony breadcrumbs in golden syrup filling a flaky textured light sweet pastry tart). Rather sadder, her compulsive behaviour worsened as she became older till she wore rubber gloves to put on the rubber gloves to clean the WC. And although bright she was foolish, she once bought a car with so little thought that when delivered she (being small like a sparrow) could not reach the pedals and had to send it straight back at serious financial loss!

Likewise when preparing to move to Norwich and leaving the farmhouse dear grandmother Amy had a bonfire made 'to clear out the attic'. A wonderful blaze, wooden trunk loads of olde papers, & odd pieces that did not burn like the others, which now I guess were parchment. How I now wonder what was lost that day.

With no hope of my grandmother running it my father and his brother Thomas had taken over the family farm after my grandfather's death just before I was born. It was already too small a farm to be economic and could never support both our family, and his brother's family, whilst they bought out both their mother and their sister Pauline, working all hours for the miserably small income it couldn't bring. They struggled as did so many small farmers, then when I reached my teens Thomas demanded his share so he could emigrate to farm in Portugal. My father gave in, sold up and took work first on another farm, and then as an agricultural store-man. Although 'failing' in the eyes of the world in many respects financially things got better then. But I get far ahead of myself.

Throughout my earlier years we really struggled as did most folk I guess. More than half the year round we were cold, perpetually hungry and always in second-hand clothes. New was a birthday or Christmas treat. Everything was hand-me-downs that barely fitted. It's hard work to trudge across a muddy field in rubber boots, harder still when these are old, perished and leaky, cut down then stuffed with newspaper to 'fit' smaller feet. Re-tailored at home mens' jackets and trousers were uncomfortable enough but recycled underpants with rubbery new elastic were plain horrible. And shortened trousers, cold and no protection.

(Why were short trousers for boys popular- because torn cloth costs money while knees will heal.)

So nearly all our clothes were pre-loved as the antique vendor might put it, hand-me-downs from family and friends. Of course those who could afford would buy from the shops, mail order barely existed, thus in the country second hand was commonplace. Rural poverty initially, then the two world wars with the cloth and clothes rationing had seen to that. This made many families handy at re-working old garments into new, long dresses into shorter, trousers with worn out knees into short trousers, the less worn margins of threadbare sheets into tea towels and handkerchiefs and so on.

I learnt to unpick jumpers, pullovers and cardigans and ball up the wool (and it was ALL wool then). With these re-cycled balls we would crochet and knit hats, scarves and squares for quilted patch-work blankets. This took quite a considerable amount of time, but then we had time in those days before the screens robbed us. Oh yes we were 'busy' but we also joked and chattered all that time so often it flew. Also there was a lot of fun in the 'dressing up' and trying on the clothes some of which were quite ancient. And you would crochet or knit when otherwise unoccupied, admittedly I was mocked for knitting in the school break by other boys who saw this as unmanly.

(At this point I must reserve a place in hell for whoever it was wrote a popular magazine article showing how to crochet boys swimming trunks from wool -without ever testing these out beforehand! The first, and only, time I wore these they immediately waterlogged, went baggy and fell off leaving me too embarrassed to come out. I have since found I was not alone! With one piece of badly thought through writing that literary fraud traumatised many of an entire generation!)

We did most 'shopping' at the many 'jumble sales' and 'bazaars' where cast offs were recycled by worthy organisations for small cash, the 'charity shops' of those days. These were great social events, usually held on a Saturday afternoon in a village or church hall. Everyone knew where the next weekends' would be and converged waiting outside for the off in huge numbers.

You would be channelled into the hall where a massive central oval doughnut of tables would be laden down with piles of clothes. And stacks of coats, sheets, blankets, and curtains and so on. The walls were ringed with another oval of tables with the shoes in piles, the bottle stall, bric a brac, unwanted (out of date -though this was not then stamped on anything) tinned food, homemade cakes and so on. It was like entering a Roman chariot race only slightly less organised and debatably not much safer. The throng would rush in a torrent grabbing at the bargains on offer with little regard to the usual civil codes. There started unbelievable scrums, physical battles would erupt between two determined matrons each holding one end of some valuable item they'd unearthed from the huge piles on the tables. The joke was they'd invented Copper wire when two of the mightiest got hold of the same dropped penny…

At most jumble sales and tables you negotiated the price with the volunteers, who of course had already sifted out the gems and put these aside for friends! The most stressful sales were extra large events where they had found their sheer scale made any pricing process rather too slow so introduced a price per bag which you filled. And everyone had bags, not plastic carriers but the original shopping bags in all sorts of materials, and often large enough to carry a small child if not three. The sheer frenzy to snatch as many bargains as possible made these giant sales quite fearsome.

Indeed children were often left playing unsupervised in the car park outside for safety!

Getting home with the spoils we'd sort them into wearable as is or material for modifying. Anything with a Zip fastener was a great prize as zips were scarce and expensive then. And such an improvement, fly buttons were slow and hard to undo, especially in the thicker woollen trousers of those days, a zip was brilliant and an easy replacement. I learned to sew, by hand and also with a foot powered Singer machine, and to do all sorts of repairs. Later in the seventies I put this to use making jeans, jackets, purses, cushions and shoulder bags all from material recovered from discarded worn out jeans. I worked on recycled carpet products including bags which were sold at Liberty's, not my design though neat and so practical I hitchhiked round half the world carrying a couple.

Quiet for once
One potent memory and tale from my early days was when I had the whole village and most of the two counties constabulary searching for me. It was the time I broke the cats' bowl. My brother was still a small infant and putting kids outside in a pram 'to air' was popular back then. He would rock the pram when left vigorously, till he was thrown out, so it had been jammed with a big box or tea chest. I hid under this trying to escape retribution for my breakage, and the more they called the stiller I became. It would have been bad enough anytime, but worse, that morning there'd been a hard frost and I had asked "Is the ice thick enough to walk on?" Panic ensued, first the local neighbours, then the county police and fire brigade, and it was not till late afternoon that my brother was taken in and my priest hole revealed.

Not that I was normally so quiet, indeed until I grasped what was going on I risked developing a Messiah complex. I seldom failed to be asking questions, why, why, why, continuously, without pause, until my worn down parents would exclaim with the classic "Jesus Christ will you shut up!" Things did not improve as I became more experimental with them uttering "Lord what are you doing now?" and then "Oh my God what ever made you do that?" An old joke but so true.

In an effort to get me out from under their feet I was first looked after by relatives in turn then when my brother added to the burden I became entrusted to an old lady in the village who 'ran a nursery'. I put this in inverted commas as it more resembled a holding pen than a modern crèche. Then every Sunday I was 'improved' by, a freezing cold, interminably long boring church service, worse sometimes yet another service after that at the other church. My father was a Church Warden and a 'High' Anglican, this involved some Catholic traditions with incense, vestments and even confessions, so he would often attend both our local village and another church over at Eye. Most Sundays I escaped the second service only by attending Sunday School when that ran. Then again after lunch I was packed off to yet another Sunday School, this one run by the local chapel. (Most village families were either church or chapel, I endured both!)

This exposure to religious diversity confused me somewhat, each claiming to have the only truth with their followers damning everyone else and their ways. I remember listening to the ladies of the village bitching over another who had not done a good enough job with the flowers... And even more horrific were the continual demands we had to try to become like the Saints- when those stories we were read of their lives described the rewards of sainthood as:

poverty, misery, starvation, imprisonment and a most painful, usually early, death as each saint was inevitably martyred in some extremely cruel and unusual way. This 'lives of saints' makes me sanguine about my children's exposure to social media, violent films and video nasties. Oddly few of these modern worries approaches the nastiness and evil in the original Grimm's Fairy stories read to me by aunts when I visited, really visceral.

Aunts and other relatives
I enjoyed being looked after by Nan and Gran, real Aunts and many 'aunts' as we called any friends of the family willing to take on a talkative little swot. For yes I realise I was an annoying talkative little pest though fortunately some of my 'aunts' were patient enough to explain some of my many queries. And much other value and learning was had from sitting under their table just listening to their gossip. I still prefer the company of women to men as I find their conversation can be more varied and interesting.
On the bright side Sundays could bring an evening trip, slow, bumpy and painful in the unpadded back of the farm Land-rover to my mother's parents, they had a small shop in Dickleburgh, a village as I mentioned only a few miles 'up' the road and visits there were one of the few opportunities when my brother and I might get sweets. And a chance to read the comics, later the newspapers, and hear Nan telling Mother tales of my Grandfather Alf's latest misdemeanours. He had met Nan as we knew mother's mother when she worked at the nearby Thelveton hall as a cook, later when she moved to another hall, Blickling I believe, in North Norfolk, he had ridden his bicycle to see her on days she had off, a round trip of sixty to seventy miles. A fit and adventurous young man Alf had tried to escape the confines of a country village by joining the Hong Kong police but had

failed their sight test. His father, Lanky Lockett, had been the local policeman for a time and publican of the Kings Head next to the church. His grandfather, Fiddy Lockett, had worked on the Norfolk wherries, settled here after meeting his wife to be visiting the long gone Zoo out on the Moor. (This survived till WWII, my mother said it was eerie hearing the howling from across the Moor at night.)
After being shot, and I believe gassed, in the Great War Alf had been forced to take up the occupation of shop assistant and then with Nan they bought the shop. To augment this Alf ran a smallholding with produce for the shop. He hated shop work and dearly loved slipping off to the horse races, the dog races and many other country pursuits. Indeed it was said he would do anything for anybody rather than what he was supposed to be doing. His days were long enough with an early rise to collect and deliver newspapers from the railway station, along with wheels of cheese, kegs of butter, chests of tea and sacks of sugar for his village store. Bizarre that such 'train delivery' was still commonplace in the late fifties. Anyway Beeching finished that all off when he closed most country lines. Before Beeching nowhere was far from a station and steam trains still ran, I remember being taken to see 'the last one' as it passed through Mellis, so noisy and smelly, I'm amazed people regret their passing!
Built originally as a pub (Queens Head) in the 15th century granddad Alf's establishment, really Nan's, was even for the nineteen fifties an old fashioned shop retaining all the fittings and much stock from a long bygone age. Downstairs remained in use much as it had always been whilst upstairs was a millinery department, long neglected, preserved exactly as when built in the days before the First World War had shattered village economies. Behind blinded windows stood a long glass fronted mahogany counter with many

compartments and along the walls rows of matching cupboards. Large drawers held all sorts of fabric and paper remnants long unusable and little drawers revealed sealing wax, pen nibs, buttons, cards, ribbons and hooks, arcane pills and powders, needles, threads and laces and so many other now forgotten things kept for no reason to not to. I remember packets of Oswego Tea (made from herbs) so old the paper was crackling to pieces, strangely memorable name.

What another wonderful place for a nosey kid. Though it was also scary, not just the dust and faded glory but a feeling of oppressiveness, made worse by the age of the building and with blocked off parts long out of use. (Although I'm sure we were never told so, it does seem to have been haunted, certainly scared me some times when I was there alone. Several folk who lived there since have asked me if I knew of anything as each in turn reported the usual weird events such as knockings and pictures flying off walls. I believe it was 'cleaned', and much rebuilt, and since then all has been quiet.)

The surrounding outbuildings were old red brick and clay lump, used for bulk storage (one smelling strongly of paraffin sold for heating and lamps, another scented with stacked boxes of soap) and the largest housing a cider press (a wooden monstrosity well beyond much possibility of ever achieving any semblance of cleanliness). As with the main shop much had been left almost untouched and undisturbed with whatever had been there unsold since the First then Second World War.

My grandparents had later purchased the orchard behind and built a small bungalow there close to their shop. Coincidentally building work started the same week as the Second World War. This was the standard seaside bungalow design but with no bathroom or toilet, these added later.

And not a Kitchen but a Scullery with a sink and boiler, and a proper pantry. My Nan preferred to do the food preparation and cooking in a shed out the back, I never understood nor was told why, another enigma.

They were always scared of thieves because of the shop takings, every door had a substantial lock, and the whole house was divided by a locking door in the middle of the central corridor. As with many folk at that time a 'front' room was kept in near perfection in its dust collecting display of seldom ever used furnishings. Indeed it was never used to my knowledge other than for receiving important visitors such as the Vicar. (My mother was supposed on one occasion to have let the family veneer fail when she let the Vicar in saying "please wait in there" then "Mum's on the khasi, would you like to see my fag cards?" (small photo-cards of famous people used as stiffening in packets of cheap cigarettes). A bathroom and toilet were later installed in half of one bedroom and a kitchen had been made from the Scullery by the time I was young enough to notice.

My favourite place was their attic, this had a wonderful wind up record player and a pile of old shellac records. I would sit up there playing favourite records over and over again such as 'With her head tucked underneath her arm', 'Will the angels play their harps for me', 'Song of the Volga boatmen', many Classical and a host of supposedly comic recordings, and some great hits such as Glen Miller. Remember, we did not even have a wireless at home at first and then listened but seldom, so this wind-up was my original major source of music. I wonder if this is why I can sing whole tunes exactly a semitone out. Or it may have been from the wheezy foot powered church and chapel organs which we sung along to.

There was something 'safe' about the attic, I never felt comfortable in the bedroom I stayed in (just cold and damp not haunted) though as I said the shop felt 'strange' at times. Similarly, my other 'silly' grandmother Amy's, farmhouse, was old and the back part far older still. (Silly is a Suffolk term for themselves for it was once Silly Suffolk, which at the time meant the county had special spiritual or religious significance, and not that they'd a dose of yokel stupidity, though ironically as mentioned Amy did indeed have a large dose of a more modern silliness, and sadly died after many years suffering Alzheimer's.) Her farmhouse also had rooms long disused and dim corridors with hanging wire operated bells that once summoned long departed servants. Particularly eerie, damp and cool was the long disused dairy come pantry which had those same bluish white washed walls as our garden loo (and just the same as used on inside walls of barns, sheds and all those outbuildings where farm chores took place).

As I said before children were expected to help in many other ways as well as feeding animals, collecting eggs, mucking out their cages and pens. Not as strong as a man a child can be nimbler and sharper eyed for tasks such as grading potatoes or just handy for turning the handle of farm machines. Stock were fed many roots such as carrots, turnips and sugar beet and these were best sliced, for which the Victorians had invented wonderful cast iron machines still in everyday use. As I said these were days before Health and Safety was considered, believe me it was tricky to operate those slicers with the constant danger of losing fingers possibly a whole arm if your attention slipped for a moment.

Our potato grader was an especially risky piece of Victorian invention with a maximum of beautifully engineered exposed gears, cogs, and moving parts to catch fingers and clothes. This was clever though, turned by hand it first cleaned, well shook the dirt off, then sieved the crop as it came from the field. The sieves took out undersized tubers leaving uniform spuds which then needed picking over by hand to remove the blemished as they passed up a ramp to the bags.

The filled bags were then raised on the most dangerous contraption I've encountered before or since, a sack hoist, that even if it had not been rusty and worm eaten, was inherently deadly. A slip or failed catch and the immensely heavy load would drop causing the winding handle to suddenly become a flailing propeller of death. This was indeed considered unsafe, so you were expected to be careful, indeed that was all part of the learning process. Likewise we helped with that other less romantic side of farming. In those days there was much more on-farm slaughtering and come Christmas there would be large numbers of birds to pluck and prepare for sale. Plucking a chicken is unpleasant work, plucking dozens is very hard and the conditions were cold and uncomfortable in a chilly shed. The smell was overpowering, and much the worse when the birds were wet, though at least wet feather fluff did not fly everywhere in choking bits as it did with dry plucking. You had to be quick, yet careful never to damage the skin as that spoiled the sale. Ducks were a tad slower to pluck than hens and a goose took half a day, plucking a goose is damn hard work believe me.

For our own use the damaged birds were seldom roasted but stewed so they could be skinned not plucked. You make an incision in the belly, and then just peel the whole outer skin off an inner membrane. You pull the skin down each leg, wing and neck then slice off at the joints. Takes a fraction of the time to pluck. Likewise with bunnies, same procedure, and for those the furry skin was worth keeping to sell.

We had turkeys a couple of times but they seemed more effort to look after and we soon gave up keeping them. Young turkeys have a death wish, seriously, they're very difficult to raise without losing most of them. And once you'd reared a percentage they were then hard to sell. A big bird they worked out rather expensive for most families, and a goose was still traditional if you could afford it. Turkey became popular later when Norfolk boy Bernard Matthews started factory farming their production on an industrial scale. (Credited with the overtly rude but adroit unofficial marketing advice "Always go for a larger older bird, she'll take more stuffing".)

Back then most people wanted their birds plucked but entire as without refrigeration they kept better that way. (Pheasants were not just kept whole but were hung by the tail till they dropped when they were reckoned ready.) A few wanted their birds eviscerating so then you had to be careful to do it neatly and separate out the heart, liver, crop/gizzard and neck, all of which were put back inside so these could be cooked to make the best gravy.

Now don't get me wrong, we did not enjoy the slaughter but a young farm boy is not squeamish, these were just more jobs that had to be done. Stock was stock for sale not pets. Meat whether for sale or the table requires slaughtering, and all the rest. But we cared deeply for those birds and animals while they were alive. I was so upset when first visiting a neighbouring farmers' 'modern' broiler unit. The hens were in a dark shed, all confined in layer upon layer of wire cages, row upon row, each cage full of miserable looking birds. Most were badly pecked and de-feathered, scarcely able to move. We kept our hens free range, ours ran about and looked happy with glossy plumage and clean combs not like those victims in that shed. That's what's so inherently wrong with much of the meat trade, it's not killing or eating meat that I see as a sin but the abuse of an animal while it's alive!

However the butchery side was but a minute part of our farm life and mostly seasonal in the run up to Christmas, for the majority of the time we were simply running messages, fetching tools or carrying lunchboxes. As we got bigger and stronger we got to do more real work, usually unpaid fruit or weed picking or if lucky on piece rate for such as hoeing weeds along with the hired men.

I learnt much country lore from Mr Bickus, semi-retired, an old horseman he stayed with us even after our horses were replaced by tractors. He introduced me to tobacco at an early age continually chain smoking counter shag, an ounce a day with an extra ounce at the weekends. (Incidentally the government allowance for growing your own tobacco, which my grandfather and many others did, was 40lbs weight a year- a colossal amount. The plants were easily grown and required much the same treatment as tomatoes.) It was Mr Bickus who taught me to sharpen my hoe. In those days the sugar beet crop needed both weeding, and thinning (before modern mono-germ seed), this was done by hand with a hoe. I was always amazed as this old boy would finish his row well ahead even though I was younger and fitter. At the end he would take a modicum of tobacco and putting it in his mouth along with a cigarette paper he proceeded to draw out a rolled cigarette which he would then light, and have a coughing attack. Then as he puffed and coughed he would take a well worn scythe-sharpening Carborundum stone from his pocket and put an edge back on his hoe. As soon as I caught up we would be off again. Well I tried to copy him, I never got the rolling in the mouth trick, I persisted and caught the smoking habit, which fortunately I managed to get away from, however I've never given up the sharpening and still pause to sharpen my hoe every so often. It is astounding what difference to your work a sharp hoe makes!

(That is something most gardening books other than mine own omit. I searched and found Percy Thrower was the last to mention sharpening hoes, indeed authors will tell you of the various forms of hoe and even repeat such foolish instructions as to walk backwards whilst hoeing, which is near impossible with a swan necked or draw hoe but once enforced in the great gardens so no footstep marks would remain visible.)

To Mr Bickus and my Grandfather Alf I owe much of my awareness of the wondrous nature all around us, to name wild flowers, know trees by their silhouette and recognise birds by their songs. Indeed they substituted for my father in many ways, it was Mr Bickus who lifted me up as an infant onto the broad back of our horses to ride bareback from the stable to the field grasping the harness for security and enjoying a spectacular view from up there (we had Shires which are very large horses, stupendously so to a small boy).

Another old farm 'boy' was Sam, he was vile in word, deed, clothes and habits, among the worst of these chewing tobacco. Putting a quid in his mouth every half hour or so he would chew, noisily suck then expectorate disgusting brown balls of stringy spit all about him. Some now complain of the widespread habit of chewing gum and of folk leaving this on pavements, also unsanitary but not as poisonous or disgusting as that tobacco spittle. Of course I tried this but gratefully never caught the habit which seems to have died out, as has the taking of snuff which many men did on occasions particularly during the coldest wettest weather. I did dabble with this on and off but as with the other habits never in front of my parents who would have been horrified. My father smoked a pipe and celebratory cigars but my mother never, indeed none of the females in my family smoked whereas almost all the men did. On asking why it seemed the tobacco ration men had received while serving in the military had guaranteed their habit even if they had been but occasional smokers before serving.

As I mentioned my Grandad Alf grew his own tobacco some of which, as ghastly and strong as his cider, I still preserve. He had an old briar pipe permanently clamped in his teeth whenever he sat down or was absorbed in some task. The only times he refrained from his pipe was when we were out hunting, for, as he said, the beasts would smell the smoke and be warned off.

I say hunting, however this was actually poaching and tobacco smoke would have alerted the gamekeepers more than the animals. Back then to start with I thought we were out in the middle of the night as that was the 'correct' time, that we were especially quiet so as not to disturb the animals or fish and that we snuck off after and never said naught to anyone as that was just the country way. I soon realised poaching was just another of those country ways. Grandad actually liked to be out at night in the dark, many of his pursuits required this and I found I liked it too, not finding it frightening nor scary, and full of interesting smells and goings on. As he said "nothing in the dark will hurt you that ain't also going to hurt in the light". At home I could seldom sneak out at night as I had to pass through my parents' bedroom. Visiting Dickleburgh became more and more welcome as I grew older. Alf would take me fishing followed by the trip before dawn or 'sparrow 'fart' as he termed it to the railway station to collect the daily newspapers. One night he taught me to pick ripe strawberries, (and other fruits) by moonlight. You cannot see red by moonlight but you can see greeny white unripe fruits, you feel for the truss, feel for a fruit you can touch but not see, it must be red and thus ripe. (Beware, dark slugs in holes in ripe fruits are also invisible…)

Alf had so many interesting smallholding ventures with cider making, tobacco curing, pigs and turkeys as well as his other 'country pursuits'. I mention cider making first, it was a very important part of the rural economy, and as there was no tax (well apparently there was, but no-one talked about it) a profitable one. For although never sold as such cider was bartered for all manner of goods and services, as I later found when I started my own production. Now to be frank Grandad's cider was not exactly prize winning, nor hygienic. (I still have some of his in jars at the back of the work-shop, black with age it has not yet mellowed.) We would collect all sorts of apples as in East Anglia we have seldom grown pure cider apple varieties. It had been found a mixture of desserts for sweetness and flavour with plenty of sharp cookers would give a drinkable if not always palatable brew. These were collected in old barrels to soften a bit then crushed to pulp with first a Victorian beet chopper then a mangle. The juicy pulp was poured into a wooden 'picture' frame covered with a piece of sacking and then this sack folded over the pulp to make a pack. A number of these packs interleaved with boards was built up in the old press which had a huge wooden screw. When this was wound down the juice would pour out to be collected in barrels where it fermented with it's own natural yeasts. Alf used to float a piece of toast spread with fresh bakers' yeast to be sure, though I doubt this had much benefit. Jokes were made you didn't need it if enough rats fell in. After a month or two the raw cider would be syphoned off the lees into fresh barrels. It would be just drinkable by Christmas but was preferred after six months or so of ageing. Thin and sharp but potent this would get you berserker drunk and was well respected/feared in the local area. I did not like it at all but loved the apple juice as this came fresh from the press. So delicious this had a hidden thorn, as it hit your stomach it would rapidly ferment, you would bloat then burp, then fart, then whoosh oh my goodness the world fell out of your bottom. Still a good clean out was deemed beneficial!

Some decades later while I was making my cider one autumn evening, to a higher quality I may add (every apple washed, rinsed, cut in quarters with every bruise, rot or grub pared off), I saw one of Alf's surviving friends wheeling past with a barrow of the blackest vilest most rotten apples. I had been warned by grandfather that this mans cider was the most evil ever –some damnation considering Alf's own productions! I asked him what he was doing with those apples and he reckoned they were good for cider as they were already fermenting...

Grandad's favourite pursuit was going to the 'nags', the horse racing at Newmarket, however this was a major trip, really not for kids so I was only taken the once. I was bored by most of it and upset we could not meet the horses though I remember his tip that the horses knew who was going to win and showed it. Sadly his betting success did not have the same certainty. His next favourite was his dogs, Lurchers for hare coursing. Again this was a bit clandestine and nowadays seen as cruel as well as illegal but as a child I was blissfully unaware of all the argument though often upset by the screaming of the hares when caught. In defence I must point out that although this was undoubtedly enjoyed as sport it was also 'for the table' as bought meat was expensive and jugged hare one of Nan's staples.

I always found hare too strongly flavoured and much preferred the rabbits we snared on other forays, and even more so that tender chicken like flesh I mentioned of our caged New Zealand White rabbits. (These were eaten at a couple of months old and not even weaned so were remarkably tender.)

Perhaps best of all was when Alf took me on fishing trips which were magical. Stealthily approaching the river or pond long before the sun rose to entice the fish to bite with first light, we baited horrible treble hooks, on a wire, required as Pike would bite through ordinary line. Then we trawled, or rather he did while I waited with a gaff to help pull the dangerous beast ashore. Although there was huge excitement when we did catch one it was mixed with grim anticipation of the meal to come as Pike flesh is both muddy and full of irritatingly sharp slender bones.

Mind you this was not as worrying a meal as the eels he trapped from the local ponds and meres. As in those days these were the receptacles for waste water and sewage from nearby dwellings (and as I write apparently are even fuller of sewage now thanks to perfidious water companies) the eels were a meal that could give rise to severe bouts of food poisoning, indeed I soon learned to avoid those with yellow bellies as these always upset my belly. Alf could and would eat almost anything though. Even small birds were good for the pies which Nan cooked for him.

Alf taught me to trap with snares, we set these for rabbits, of course this was definitely poaching and more risky as the evidence had to be left and returned to frequently. I became adroit at setting the ring of slippery wire just over a run hidden with whisps of dried grass. The trick was the bunny would be moving quickly along the run in the open and be snared whereas other animals such as cats moving more slowly would not often be caught. It distressed me so much when one was trapped and had to be dispatched. Even worse was when my pet cat Tid came home with a rear leg skinned down to the bone by a crueller trap, we traced her trail back a half mile then lost it crossing the old rail line, bless her trusting we would help her when all we could do was a kindness with a shotgun.

Shooting parties
Alf seldom shot, perhaps expediently as in the quiet of the countryside this would have alerted the gamekeepers too easily. However later once tall enough to pass muster he would take me to join organised forays for the local estates as an extra beater. When you see photos of old hunting parties note the baggy clothes beaters wore –partly for warmth, partly so they could slip 'lost' pheasants or other winnings inside. You then had difficulty hobbling home unnoticed with one dripping inside each of your trouser legs. Pheasant and partridge were seen as good tucker and a bit of a feast though as with most game I found their flavour too strong.

Pheasants were reared on the local estates much like chickens and then released. Very dim these would wander about quite lost if not bagged by the series of shooting parties. These pheasants would sometimes take up home with your hens (and can cross apparently) and wait to be fed, foolish as they were worth a few bob. Out in the woods they roost at night and you can spot the branches by the droppings underneath, same for pigeons though they roost higher up. If those branches were low enough we would go back at night, sneak up, one from in front with a small torch to attract their attention from afar and to illuminate them, the other to grab them from behind.

We had wild ducks on the farm ponds in winter, these were rather greasy, not very plump fleshed and too strongly flavoured. Oddly we seldom farmed duck. Wild geese were occasionally got and not much better eating than the ducks.

As with ducks farmed white geese were reckoned much better eating than the wild but far too valuable for their eggs for us to afford to eat them. Wood pigeons were much less common in those days and were taken anytime seen, save when the Ivy was in berry as it was said this made their flesh poisonous.

(I blame the awful murders at Dunblane for the massive increase in wood pigeons. In a knee jerk reaction politicians banned hand-guns and further, more onerously, restricted the owning of rifles. Now a .22 bullet is a lot less costly than a 12 bore cartridge and does not leave many nasty bits of shot, thus shooting with a rifle kept the pigeons saleable. Since the value of pigeons was low this change made shooting them unprofitable, so they've been left to breed and are now in plague proportions…)

Sparrows on the other hand have decreased, once they were about in vast numbers, when our hens were fed these descended in droves and were driven away to let the hens feed. We would trap them in wire cages as a dozen or so would make a pie, tiny morsels with more bones than flesh this was a tasty if fiddly meal. (When I started gardening back at Dickleburgh I re-discovered Alf's old wire cage trap so used this to catch some sparrows, which were then still bothersome, not for pies but to feed my cats. I remember one friend looking for something in my freezer and opening a tub found it stuffed full of little frozen birds, she was quite upset by them.)

Most birds were nearly all seen as outright pests or food or both, and from an early age I became a good shot. I started with an air rifle and also a 9mm garden gun. This latter was not really for shooting birds, the many pieces of shot rendered them risky eating, but for killing rats. I'm sad now how many poor birds were killed and injured by my 'practising'. Indeed I stopped shooting for 'sport' the day I failed a clean shot and wounded a Hedge Betty which fluttered onto a nearby roof where it slowly died accompanied throughout it's suffering by it's grieving mate, I still feel so guilty and sad about that I've never gone hunting since.

One bird we set out to shoot and seldom ate on the farm were Rook squabs. Rooks are similar to Crows (if you see a rook on it's own it's a crow, several crows together will be rooks) and these were then misguidedly seen as serious pests needing control though we now know they do more good than harm. The adults were trapped in rook traps, large wood and wire netting half open cages with a funnel shaped part open roof. Once used to coming for the bait the trap sides would be added and the next visit they could get in to find no escape. However adult Rooks are too strongly flavoured unless you are really desperate. The young squabs however are less gamey, even so we only ate their breasts in pies.

These squabs were to be had for a few weeks only each year by shooting them from underneath in their rookery trees. They emerged from their nests to sit on a branch nearby as their wings strengthened enough to fly. At this stage they were sitting ducks and easily shot. One wrinkle the old boys never warned you was never to shoot from directly underneath. We used .22 rifles with hollow point bullets, these splayed out on contact and gave a surer kill. The point was to fire up at an angle, if you fired straight up from underneath then the guts which were blown out went straight up, and straight down again, covering you in a most unpleasing gory mess. You only did that once, the others' laughter was all part of your initiation rite.

A rifle was much the preferred gun for shooting food to eat because as I said of the cost of ammo and the annoyance of bits of shot in the meat (you could break a tooth on a bit of shot). However a rifle is good only if you can take a clear or clean shot of a stationary target. When the game is moving the 12 bore with it's spray of shot was more likely to bring the prey down though often not giving such a sure kill, and with much less chance at any range. Thus the use of dogs to fetch the fallen bird or game, these would usually be retrievers as their name suggests though seldom pure breeds and more often mongrels. One of the commonest crosses in E. Anglia was our local Lurchers, themselves hybrids between Greyhounds and other breeds. Lurchers were particularly wanted for running down rabbits and hares. They had the useful nature of being curled up snoozing whenever not required, unlike more active breeds which would be harder to secrete under the sacks in the back of the van and could give the game away if stopped by a gamekeeper.

My favourite Lurcher Poppy only became mine as she was deemed useless for hare coursing. She was very quick but had lost her tail as a puppy so could not make fast turns without tumbling thus she seldom caught much. I miss those early morning walks through damp meadows with Poppy bounding off and eventually returning. Twas she who gave me the trick of looking innocent when out checking snares, all I had to do was carry her lead, if stopped I'd ask if they'd seen my dog who I was searching for...

One day I came home from school to see a couple of rabbits lying by the front door, it was a gift from another farmer but it got me thinking. I imagined crossing a lurcher with a retriever or sheep dog then training the pups to go off hunting on their own for bunnies and then to bring them home and stack them by the door. I liked the idea of a stack they would maintain, if it got smaller they'd just go off and get a couple more. Meanwhile of course I'd be selling bunnies.

I said Poppy was no good for hare coursing as she had no tail. But turned out she was valuable for breeding and the original owners wanted her back, we foxed several attempts to steal her. However one day she disappeared, but then so did so many of my favourite pets. At the time I did not suspect foul play but now I wonder, as I mentioned my parents were caring but not loving. It did seem each animal I showed affection for would suddenly die or disappear. But then death was part of the country life, it did not seem such an unnatural thing, after all we killed hens and stock and shot to eat.

Fox hunting though was never much pursued in our part of East Anglia. There were few foxes anyway because the large estates employed gamekeepers to keep these, and badgers and birds of prey controlled in order to conserve their pheasants and partridges for shooting parties. Anyway most of us thought fox-hunting was a pretty damn foolish thing as you could not eat the fox nor sell it's pelt for very much, and after going to all that effort to catch it. I have no love for foxes though, one mauled our hens to death when I was young. I discovered the disaster when taking the morning feed to them. Foxes do not just kill to eat, they slaughter all about them then take but one away to consume. Their carnage is appalling, bits of hen, feathers and blood sprayed all over the inside and more spread in the run outside the hens' hut.

Back in those childhood days deer were seldom seen, we knew some were in Thetford Forest a half day bike ride distant but never saw one locally whereas now they're more common. Especially the dwarf Muntjac and similar Chinese Water deer, both simply unknown back then and now almost everywhere. Introduced in relatively recent times these had not spread to our area in my youth, these are the better eating of the deer family somewhat resembling pork -

so if any had appeared back then they sure would not have survived long.

However there was another critter which I saw only the once and they've now gone, fortunately as they were undermining the banks of the Broads. A sally further down the Waveney towards the Broads would reveal their huge burrows holing the banks. These were the work of Coypu, a South American escape much resembling a gigantic beaver. This was considered a prize, the meat was dark and strong resembling ox-tail and not popular. However these were sought after because their fur was readily sold, reputedly for much more than we got for our usual rabbit pelts, they were considered a pest and have now been extinguished here.

a cruel deed
Rabbits had been the poor countryman's standby since Norman times, illicit but easy these were everywhere and many landowners turned a blind eye to hungry men stealing rabbits. Of course during the Wars the bunnies achieved serious cash value for their meat which became worth as much as their pelts, local lads had weekly taken loads to the cities to sell off-the-ration. Plus, during and since the war many more people had started keeping rabbits for their own table and some sold surplus locally as well. Naturally folk did not want to stop eating rabbit as it was inexpensive. The butchers were envious of this competition which was vying with them even more after rationing ceased as sales could then be openly done. Thus somehow someone procured a diseased rabbit, probably from Australia where a nasty infectious virus had been used to eliminate rabbits. This was deliberately let loose near the south coast and the virus spread like wildfire. It was said cruelly thoughtless people were collecting sick rabbits to release on their own

farms as they regarded rabbits as a pest. The ghastly germ warfare spread across the country in but a few months leaving a trail of seriously sick slowly dying bunnies hobbling about everywhere, falling into roads and unable to find their way off.

Myxamotosis damages the rabbits' nervous systems leaving them with swollen blinded eyes unable to find food or water so they die very slowly and presumably painfully.

At first we noticed the odd one, then they were hobbling all around, day and night, it was a sad sight. We would put the poor things out of their misery but there were too many to 'priest' even a small proportion. No bunny was safe, even pets in cages in buildings succumbed as the virus reached them, somehow on fodder or whatever (apparently it was spread by fleas).

Rabbits became fewer so poaching them soon became near pointless, especially as people feared buying a 'myxied' one. In theory myxied bunnies were safe to eat if cooked but few tried, knowingly, often they were too emaciated anyway. Rabbits had also been very cheap food for dogs so these became much more expensive to keep.

Alf was certainly a dog lover. He allegedly kept a dog under his bed in hospital after being injured in the war, often disobedient but talented he was promoted and demoted after taking a squad of fellow soldiers to the races, where he was seen by his officers. My Nan was not a great dog lover, she liked them but not in her home. Thus he was obliged to keep his coursing lurchers round a friends (rather conveniently the local butchers). When she passed away he soon had some home and in his latter days kept Whippets. These are small greyhounds, very nimble and fast, totally psychotic pursuing anything that moves, immediately killing anything that cannot move faster.

It was this that led to our falling out in his very last years. I was in my early teens when Nan died and thereafter each Sunday he would come to us for a meal, bringing his whippet with him. At that time I had an old very fat and dearly loved cat Engelbert. Each Sunday Grandad would park on the drive, get out and let his whippet out the back, immediately it would rush round excitedly and too often my dear moggy dozing in the sun would have to rocket up the nearest tree or be trashed. After many attempts at getting him to put the dog on a lead before letting it out I gave him the ultimatum "If your bloody dog kills my cat I'll shoot the damn mutt!" We did not speak again maintaining that long country tradition of in-family quarrels and feuds.

Indeed it was only as he lay dying in hospital that I relented, I motorcycled through a storm to get there, sat by his bed and asked his forgiveness then chatted for a while more as he completely ignored me. A nurse came in and said "Would you like me to try and wake him?" He had been 'asleep' with his eyes open all the time, which explained his stony refusal to give me his blessing. He was sadly comatose and never recovered thus we parted un-reconciled. I grieved more over his parting than I did later for my father.

But I get ahead of myself again.

Death though sad did not seem such a trauma in country areas being accepted as the concomitant to having a life and was actually feared less than serious injury which would leave you destitute and a burden to others. Perhaps this sanguinity was because so many people were seriously disfigured or disabled from the two World Wars (or one war with a break for Germany to recover as Alf had put it). This was when I first met 'drug addicts', people thought to be more a recent urban or metropolitan problem. However in the fifties and sixties there were men who were drug dependent living in our village though these were not at all like 'modern' junkies. These were men who had become hooked on opiate painkillers whilst recovering from some dreadful wartime injury. They were spoken of in hushed compassionate terms and regarded with little opprobrium. They would get their 'medication' from the doctor and as long as they took it lived otherwise normal lives, well as normal as their injuries allowed. It is generally thought that country folk are hostile and narrow minded to anyone 'different' but their compassion for these victims was exemplary.

Intolerance is an odd thing, 'foreigners' were not people of a different cast or hue if they were 'local' but definitely folk coming from the next county but one, and anyone vaguely metropolitan, was the devil incarnate. Trevor Phillips when the racial equality supremo commented to the effect that people of colour were not welcome in country areas. The ignorant townie! NO strangers of any extraction have ever been immediately welcome in country districts as with many centuries of experience we suspect, nay know, they've probably come with ill intent.

What is even odder it seems Trevor may not have known the wartime experience of East Anglia. Although the middle of East Anglia was and is the middle of nowhere just for a very few years at the end of WWII when my parents were young there were large numbers of 'Yanks' here concreting over our farmlands which were so conveniently flat for building airfields. Ironically my parents' generation became exposed to the Jim Crow laws of these American invaders. Surrounded by airfields positioned every few miles each of these were built then guarded by racially divided troops which were housed and allowed out separately. Both the nearby towns of Diss and Eye were designated as open for Afro-American servicemen only while other places beyond

Eye such as Harleston to the coast were off limits to them this area being reserved for whites only.

Perhaps odder still was the apparent acceptance of gender diversity, something we also think of as so 'modern'. In the nearby market town was a fish merchants. A great slab of marble projected out into the street covered in crushed ice to display what fishy wares could be obtained, welcome with so many other shortages before and after rationing. This was run by a couple. She had slicked down short hair and a black suit, white shirt, tie and polished brogues. She had been a bulldozer driver in the womens' land army and was thickset and muscular. He was slight with a dapper air, bouffant hair, flouncy shirt, silk cravat and neat suit under the white apron. All this mattered not a whit for they were talkative and kind and friendly, and tolerant of children giving us bits of ice to suck (oh how Health & Safety would frown on this now, ice with raw fish sauce!)

Indeed Health & Safety were concepts that just had not then made it very far into the sticks. One of the towns' butcher shops was quite the middle ages film set, a clay lump building with brick floor, those ubiquitous bluish lime washed walls and a wooden chopping block apparently set there just before the Crusades. Raw carcasses hung from beams on hooks with little separation from the dripping feathered and furry game brought in. Refrigeration was absent, washing facilities apparently likewise. I cannot be sure but suspect their toilet was no more than a hole in the floor of a lean-to emptying into the large pond next door. (Known as the Mere this huge sinkhole come effluent catchment was once reputed to be the Devil's Hand-basin, a name now only remembered by the sign on a garage and petrol station in an outlying village. This Mere was also the main source of Alf's somewhat risky yellow bellied eels eaten when other meats were short.)

Another remarkable, and remarkably tiny, shop was the town tobacconist. No larger than a small garden shed this had been there for countless generations tended in my youth by two old sisters in black smock like dresses each with a remarkable resemblance to grandmother in the Giles cartoons. (If you don't know of these look the annuals them up, much of my early knowledge of politics, social lore and recent history came from reading a collection of his annual compilations kept in Nan's toilet.)

Commercial ready made cigarettes had become most smokers' preference and far outsold other older products with a proliferation of brands at the front of the wee counter and on the shelves nearby. Inside the glass cases and on higher shelves rested packets, tins and boxes of cigars, rolling tobacco and pipe mixtures unsold for decades. I would stand transfixed by the packaging as my Grandfather watched them weigh out his favourite pipe tobacco from black Chinoisery jars. (Alf thought his home grown tobacco fine for everyday but not good enough for Sunday afternoons after Church.) One cigarette packet design that still lingers in my memory was Passing Clouds which had a facsimile oil painting on the front of a cavalier enjoying his smoke. Probably no older than Victorian in origin this was a mere youngster compared to some of the forgotten brands of bundles of leaves and blends held just in case of a sale one day. The greatest number were pipe tobacco, varieties so strong even the wartime shortages had not made them palatable, especially as in the area so many grew their own tobacco. Far older still were the clay pipes, these had long been superseded by briar, metal and Bakelite pipes and so were kept high up on the topmost shelves out of harms way wrapped in tissue paper with just one or two in the front window on dusty display. Most curious of all were churchwardens, small bowled pipes with a two to three foot long narrow arching stem. So long and so delicate it is no wonder bits of broken stems are often found in old gardens.

Born in 1953 not 1903
Now if all so far has sounded as I said as if I was born into the early nineteenth century, remember this was the '50s becoming the '60s, nuclear bombs, jet planes and television had arrived, elsewhere. However things moved so slowly out in these hinterlands. In fact in many ways my early life was little different to that over the centuries before. There were still blacksmiths working their forges, though not so much for horse-shoes as a travelling farrier was more the job for those. Smithies were visited for repairs to various bits of farm equipment and especially hand tools such as rakes and hoes.

And for many years horses were still about pulling traps into town on market day, sadly tractors finally ousted working horses while I was still small. Indeed we were nearly the last farm to use working horses in the area. It was awful when told they were going, I'd so enjoyed being with them. I'd been allowed near the horses when they were standing around being refitted or between tasks as they were so gentle. I was always pestering to be near them and was allowed to hang around so got to watch my father and the men do many jobs. With tractors it changed, a man worked on his own with tractor and implement, and even back then this was seen as not very safe for little kids to be near.

While we still had horses on the farm I'd watched the corn in the field mown with a horse pulled cutter and binder that clacked and rattled round the fields. It was bundled into sheaves to ripen in the field, stooked up over wooden frames to dry and ripen after cutting, then transported to a stack to be threshed by a travelling steam driven outfit. This had been built with more of that Victorian ingenuity and was still in use simply because it still did the job. The sheaves were thrown onto a rising conveyor dropping and disappearing into a whirling machine which with unremitting noise and smoke produced a stream of grain run into large sacks. These sacks of grain were then stored in barns in great mounds three deep. (That damn dangerous sack hoist machine was in use again.) The threshing machine was 'modernised' with the belching smelly coal fired steam engine which had also pulled it from farm to farm replaced by big old truck and a mesmerising Lister stationery engine running on oil. This spun a pulley driving a great big belt to the threshing machine, it ran rhythmically with a wonderful rumbling thump thump, thump thump, thump thump. This machine was water cooled, an open steaming chamber of water surrounded the barrel and needed topping up as the water boiled away (and was used for boiling eggs lodged in the top for hot snacks).

Our farm slowly modernised and as I approached teenage years a second hand combine harvester was bought, another huge noisy machine which cut and processed the corn in one go in the field. The cereal crops were reeled in at the front, cut off remarkably uniformly at ankle height (this stubble was horrid to walk through), the grains separated from stalks and chaff which were belched out the back. On these early versions the grain was run into sacks on a platform on the side of the harvester where a second man worked changing and tying these when filled to feed them down a slide onto the field. These sacks were then collected heaved onto a trailer and carried to the barns. The straw was wanted for bedding the stock so another machine, a baler, was driven along collecting and packing it into just moveable wads bound with twine which were stacked for winter. Once we'd collected it all we ran hens on the stubble after to glean the missed grains. Often on many farms though the straw was burnt where it lay, along with so many tiny critters, and a whole load of the fertility, insane waste.

The pace was gathering and the modern world had come over the horizon, quite literally for through the background of wind and birds would come a rushing and roaring as another jet plane flew over low. Every so often a sonic bang would be heard in the distance out over the North Sea. Cars and trucks were more frequently on the roads.

But I get far ahead of myself again.

My parents made improvements as they could. When my younger brother was born our house had electric lights fitfully replacing paraffin lamps and candles and water soon arrived by pipe. By the time I was eight or so the lean to kitchen was replaced by a brick built one and we had a bath-room with flushing toilet.

One treasured memory from the changeover was playing in the new kitchen cupboards under the new sink at which my mother was engaged when my younger sibling ran in screaming all covered with blood. Now he had been continually up to mischief and being junior had successfully shifted the blame for many misdemeanours onto my shoulders. Mother cried out asking what on earth had happened. And not seeing me concealed in the half closed cupboard he bleated "Robert hit me with the saw mummy!" Mother repeated her question as she cleaned his wound, he again blamed me. At last mother realised how I had been fitted up, and looking back perhaps rather often before. My brother was never believed so wholeheartedly again. Fortunate not very long after he attempted auto-lobotomy sticking the metal rod axle from a toy truck up his nose all the way to the end stopped by the second wheel still attached. He also tried to pin this on me but his word had rightly become suspect.

Happiest days?
Aged five I had been handed over to the local primary school. My mother had taught me the basic 3Rs –'Reading, riting, rithmetic' especially giving me a love of reading, thankfully, and we read books at home first together then on my own. My mother, who had been an assistant teacher after the war then worked as a telephonist. (In those days phone calls went through a manual switching exchange unless they were very local, or on the party line where you could talk, or just listen, to the neighbours who shared the same.) As she had already taught me the rudiments, to count, read and write, so I was sat at the back of the class whilst those more in need were concentrated upon. These were hard work for the teachers as tasteless jokes about country folk's incest, and unusual finger and toe counts, were not then libellous or misrepresentative. There existed long established 'country ways' with inadvertent inbreeding between near relatives if not actual incest which had still not been eradicated. Plus added to this for centuries most of the brightest and fairest had left for the cities.
Favourably the local Primary was one of the few new buildings in the area and so was 'modern' ie had fitting windows and central heating. Oh I loathed being away from home, hated being inside all day, but how I loved the warmth. I learned to hog radiators and would sit with my back to one whenever possible if not actually, forbiddingly, sitting on them.
The school was divided into two age groups, one for each teacher, with less than a dozen kids in each, 5-8 and 8-11. By the time I had finished the first stint I'd read every book on the shelves (I was encouraged to read just to keep me

quiet!) and had, with special permission, started on the books in the upper class' library). By the time I left I had read near every book in the school (not so great a task as it should be). And I had started on the town library in Eye. An imposing Victorian edifice this was fearsome looking though turned out welcoming. Though technically too young I was introduced by an aunt and encouraged to borrow books, and could not believe my luck. So many to choose from. Could I read them all? Once again I get ahead of myself.

Mother also taught piano to other kids, and one of her learning tricks with us was 'guess the composer' when she would play pieces of music while we worked out who had written the piece. Another of her ploys as we became older was to give prizes for answering quiz questions on the wireless and later the TV. Sweets initially then much appreciated cash as we grew older. I remember correct answers for Top of the Form were four a penny, later on University Challenge arrived and answers were a penny each (not much considering their difficulty).

Sadly my primary school was apparently not very good, despite the appearance of modernity the 'head' teacher was so appalling I failed the 11 plus exam. This exam was to determine which secondary school I was to go to. My parents could not believe I'd failed so they appealed. At an interview I presented some of my fossil collection and cards of bleached bones extracted from owl pellets. I won the last place over my competitor who took his stamp collection and cigarette cards.

(It was later realised my schools' head teacher had for a long time been not just under-performing but hopelessly so. I gather no child taught by her passed the 11 plus during any of the previous fourteen years!!! I doubt this could happen now but back then most folk just kowtowed and accepted authority figures no matter how inept or self important they appeared. Plus expectations were low, country kids were thought destined to be clod hoppers aspiring muck rakers and tractor drivers.

Luckily the lack of the due schooling did not matter much as I nearly always had my head stuck in a book and to be fair I was a disruptive child. Far too clever for my own good, and often resenting inadequate teaching I would naively 'talk back' when offered obviously duff information or foolish advice. This does not make you popular, few folk like having their ignorance displayed nor their prejudices shot down by a precocious child.

Sports were another anathema, I just did not 'get' either the sense of organised sport nor feel any 'team ethos'. Being expected to do so many farm and household chores plus walk or cycle to school meant many of us country kids really did not need extra exercise as perhaps town and urban children might. Anyway it was all a bit pointless as sport was not taught, merely supervised. It was as though we were automatically imbued with knowledge of the games, their rules and tactics. I still do not know how to play most of them.

I also suspect my Primary head teacher more than disliked me and my bookish ways and gave me a hard time deliberately. One afternoon reluctantly playing (without understanding) cricket she made me field so close in to the batsman I was smashed in the face by the bat. In those days accidents were not noted, not even much acted upon, so despite dripping blood I was chastised for being a wimp. I still have difficulty breathing through one nostril from the damaged nose I sustained that day.

School dinners were a mixed blessing. I was permanently hungry, made more acute by my younger brother demanding equal portions of everything at home, he even had our baked beans (a much liked but seldom bought treat) counted out to ensure fairness. Despite my being older feeding the same to both of us resulted in my brother outgrowing me and by the time I went to secondary school he was already larger, taller, heavier and by far my physical superior.

The major drawback with the school meal was each pupil was served at a hatch, you got what you were given then obliged to eat everything regardless, rationing was only just over and food was precious. This was no problem most days as we were hungry but we all lived in dreaded anticipation of some meals, the quality of food sold to schools was not exactly as it should have been. I still remember being held back to finish a plate of over-boiled cabbage with a piece of liver so tough, gristly and basically un-chewable thus un-swallowable that I slipped it into a tin of powder paint when teachers' back was turned. Perversely she must have known it was inedible as she cross questioned me as to what I had done when I said I'd finished it!

Likewise a very mixed blessing we were fortunate in having a daily milk ration, certainly a good idea from the point of view of nutrition. However here the problem was older bottles were logically to be consumed before the newer, but remember refrigerators were still scarce so the bottles just sat outside the classroom slowly fermenting. Many days we were obliged to gulp down rancid milk so many days gone over it had separated.

Although the teaching was inadequate I do remember some subjects and tasks were still enjoyable. I recently found some of my school exercise books, bound and decorated by ourselves, in which my drawings reveal the direction I was heading. (My father had been an excellent artist but had mostly given up after entering the army). It is my nature studies that showed my early interest with many drawings of plants and animals accompanying my somewhat imaginative text. My story book, where we choose a picture cut from a magazine to write about, abounds with cats and gardens, still two of my favourites. I was recently proudly showing these to a retired editor who pointed out that a few of that teacher's 'corrections' were actually incorrect...

We seldom had lessons that inspired, indeed most were lacking in both content and delivery, teaching aids other than blackboard and chalk were unknown and we wrote as told with ink pens dipping or refilling these in ink wells set in the desks (the new fangled Biros were still too expensive). Many of us had blue fingers from leaky pens and blue tongues from licking the nibs, I doubt that ink was actually safe to imbibe, goodness knows what was in it. School trips out were mostly on foot either rambling on Mellis common or pond dipping which I found fascinating, and church services which I already had my fill of! Likewise the most frequent school visitors were priests who failed to teach the love of a god but threatened us all with burning in hell if we were ever to indulge in any of an innumerable number of mostly unspecified sins the performing of which we were left to guess at. (One day myself with a few others were punished for having been caught looking at the half naked bodies of some native peoples in the sole copy of National Geographic the school held.)

Physical punishment was still the norm back then, inattention, talking, talking back and other minor infractions were dealt with by a flying piece of chalk, or worse by a flung board rubber (a thick piece of wood wrapped in felt). Clips and smacks to the hands, and on top of the head, were common. For worse crimes the punishment rose to having the back of your legs slapped with a measuring stick. For the most serious crimes the cane was still used, I suspect with malice, forethought and deliberation. Downright perverted now I look back. I was lucky for somehow I managed to avoid getting caned! Worse, the fear was if you told your parents you'd been punished unfairly for something and they dared complain you would likely receive another dose, we all learnt to keep schtum. Bizarrely such treatment was commonplace and apparently relished by some part of the population for there was even a popular TV show called 'Whacko' starring a head teacher making then taking every opportunity to inflict pain with a cane to childrens' behinds. Ah, as they says, "the good old days..."

Abuse came from many directions. People considered it quite acceptable to beat another's child for any transgression whatever, even if no grave sin had been committed. I remember a sustained slapping I received from one mother when her offspring accused me, rather unjustly, of having stolen one of his badges. True I was taunting him with it after I picked it up off the ground where he'd dropped it, it was hardly sneakily thieving for I was waving it around. And even if I had actually stolen it to keep would knocking me half senseless have been appropriate? The same family also had a vicious black cur that introduced me to my first dog-bite. My parents never protested about that either, for that family were 'more respectable' as their father had a 'proper job' with a suit and tie, and one just did not 'question' such people.

Everyone was so obsessed with class and position even though two world wars had supposedly finished the class system off. Likewise the local doctor seemed oblivious to, or enjoyed, children's pain. He abandoned me halfway through an injection to answer his telephone leaving me holding this huge, heavy, glass and metal re-usable hypodermic (with a needle so large it belonged in a veterinary museum) stuck in my arm. But I'd really rather not dwell on such painful memories.

Brutality and beastliness were everywhere, perhaps rife because two appalling wars were still recent and dulling people's concerns. Especially in Norfolk which battalions suffered the worst Japanese atrocities having first survived the German's efforts. Such horrific stories seemed to have dulled everyone to smaller crimes. Thus perverts and paedophiliacs were able to act without heed as no-one would or could, believe a child versus an adult, and particularly any as 'respectable' as teachers, doctors and priests.

We may complain of the nanny state interfering in family affairs but surely this is better than those horrors that were so prevalent and which went unseen and uncorrected. Especially horrific was how a child was not believed because of 'unquestioning' acceptance, when "one of our betters" was implicated, particularly when serious abuse was involved.

On the stage

There were bright moments. I remember one winter when our school held the Christmas 'show' for the parents. Many kids were off sick, I think it was mumps that time as before the vaccination campaigns we all suffered that, and Measles, German measles, Chicken pox, Whooping cough, Flu' of course, even Diphtheria, all went the rounds, I had all bar the last. These are now uncommon ills, praise be. (If you are considering not having your children vaccinated take it from a survivor, these diseases are not minor but very unpleasant potentially serious afflictions!) Anyway my brother and I were the stars of the show, well almost the only intact performance, singing 'There's a hole in my bucket' with my brother taking the male and I the female part. Perhaps it was that afternoon I got to love being 'on stage' tasting applause for the first time.

Although my early schooldays were bleak bordering on harsh we knew little else. Television had only just arrived in the sticks, after all this needed mains electricity a massive aerial and not to be too far from the early transmitters. I first saw TV at my grandparents who got one to watch the races as Alf so loved the nags and acted ('unofficially') as a bookies runner. Once he nearly lost house and shop by keeping back a bunch of bets on the Grand National favourite which he'd had a sure tip would take a fall but which then won).

We had a wireless (radio), nothing like a modern one as it had valves that glowed in the dark and required huge battery packs the size of a stack of books. There were few stations and listening time was limited by the need to conserve the expensive batteries. Both my Aunt Bertha and Grandmother Amy had mains radios, these were listened to for specific programs and never left turned on in the background. I remember Aunt Bertha always listened to Gardeners Question Time, which rather ironically I found 'boring'. 'Listen with mother' was of course obligatory. Actually I found most radio programs boring and preferred to read. I was fortunate, as I said, for when visiting my grandparents I could read the comics in their shop (being careful so they could be sold after) and as I grew curious graduated to newspapers in my continual search for more material.

Some have remarked how honest everyone was back then and how lovely it must have been to leave your doors and windows open and never locked even at night. (Yet my grandparents were perpetually in fear of robbery.) Anyway what would any thief have stolen? Like most folk we had bugger all and what we did have was old and worn out. (Bugger is an East Anglian term we often utter, probably a reduction of bugbear, possibly Bulghar for Genghis Khan's horsemen who had terrorised Europe, and is not taken as referring to a sexual act. Naturally in a country area there remained a whole local dialect with terms such as 'on the huh' for being aslant or askew, 'thas a rummun' for that's interesting. This in addition to the soft accent. It's said no true East Anglian can pronounce chimney unless coached as invariably it comes out chimmley. Despite my acquired 'radio pronounced' English I lapse into soop for soup & soap, roattes for roots and trulle for trowel unless I'm careful and sober.)

Toys, no, play-things
My younger brother and I were left to roam free, unfettered by todays' paranoid standards. Adult supervision was not seen as essential once you were no longer an infant and anyway every one was busy. Thus often we wandered about and poked our noses into every corner of farm and village, in every semi-derelict house and falling down shed (of which there were many as back then gentrification had not arrived). As well as father's wagon and the old garage I've mentioned derelict barns offered much interest with worn out wagons, broken machinery and vast piles of worn out and discarded tools.

As we got older we ventured further to friends' farms and to the other end of the village where there was a playground. This was a joy for although old and worn this was post Victorian engineering at it's best. A marvellous top shaped merry go round, immensely heavy but huge fun was first choice. The swings were brilliantly made from a solid reliable long lasting point of view, but we all had ones of rope and a bit of plank at home so found these rigid iron and wood boxes hanging on iron chains a tad cold and less comfortable. There was a tall brass slide so burnished by countless bottoms you could see your face in it. A substantial see saw and a circular spinning seat / platform. These disappeared one by one, I don't know whether it was wear and tear, rising insurance or health and safety but by my teens most had gone leaving a large hole in our village kids' summer evening entertainments.

Naturally in wet weather we would sneak into the barns and sheds. Behind the main farm barns way across the fields was a 'modern' Dutch barn (a roof with no sides) which sheltered massive stacks of hay and straw bales. The hay was dried grass from the meadows for winter feed, the straw the stems of wheat or barley used for bedding. Barley was the softer but had many awns which are prickly thin bits attached to the grains, the wheat was kinder to the skin. We were forbidden to play there as falling bales could have seriously injured us but of course we did even excavating dens deep inside. (Good job we never tried smoking there!) We also made our own slides; wisps of straw on a sloping bed of bales are nearly as slippery as water. Other than the odd rebuke we got away with this until one day when my brother and I collided where two slides crossed, my jaw crashed down onto his head with such force several of my front teeth were chipped, simultaneously removing the tip of my tongue. This did grow back but the damage to my teeth was more serious. The local dentist smoothed the jagged edges with an antique, under-powered, drill with insufficient painkillers almost punishing me for my foolishness.

But enough of that, as I was becoming aware a 'new world' was evident even out in the sticks with cars and telephones becoming commonplace, water and electric in most homes and eventually televisions. You may not believe me but outdoor bucket toilets were still in regular use as late as the 1980s when South Norfolk still had a dozen houses it was obliged to regularly visit to empty with the council 'honey wagon'.

Television was the game changer, it showed the rest of the world in a way books and radio had not. Mind you it was only one, later two channels, and these were available for just a small part of the evening. TV showed different lifestyles and changed ours, until TV we did indoor chores, whistled and sang, and played card and board games. Once TV arrived we began to sit just watching, a very different form of family interaction, perhaps not all for the good in the end. I rather suspect people from the generations before had sharper mental skills from the parlour games they played. Of course I may be wrong and it may not be TV, or now the internet and social media to blame, for perhaps it was actually the fault of going metric?

I grew up knowing temperatures in degrees Fahrenheit, weight by stones, pounds and ounces, size in yards, feet and inches and money in pounds, shillings and pence. And these kept you mentally nimble.

(16oz made a pound weight, 14lb a stone, 8 stone or 112lb a hundredweight, cwt, or one twentieth of a ton. A cwt sack of anything was as much as a strong man could carry, a half cwt one he could comfortably carry.

12 inches made a foot, 3 feet a yard and 1760 yards a mile. 12 pennies made a shilling, 2 shillings a florin, 2 shillings and 6 pence made a half crown, 20 shillings, 10 florins or 8 half crowns made a pound, plus we had halfpennies, three-penny bits and six pence coins as well, farthings had gone before I came along but were still about, had a Wren embossed on the back if I remember rightly.)

Sure Metrics were easier to calculate but the corollary was we no longer needed to stretch our brains every time we bought or measured something. Calculating in our heads how much a number of goods cost for a price per given weight or size was a feat of long division and multiplication managed by almost everyone for the simple reason we had to. Then we had to do even more mathematics to work out if the change received was correct.

(Just try this- we want to buy a stone of potatoes at sixpence halfpenny per pound = 14 x 6.5 which is 91 pence, so divide this by 12 to get the cost of 7 shillings and 7 pence. Now if we handed over a pound we need change of 20 less 7 plus 1 shillings plus 12 minus 7 pence, that is 12 shillings and five pence for which we might receive 12 one shilling coins, or 6 florins or 4 half crowns plus a three-penny bit and two pennies. And that was an easy one!

Pocket calculators were not yet invented so every shopping trip made both customer and assistants without a clever till perform multiple arithmetical tasks- surely of benefit to keeping our minds active and supple. Don't get me wrong, I am not against the change to Metrics but speculate it caused unnoticed collateral damage.

I was good at simple maths anyway, indeed many subjects were not that difficult for me as I'd read so widely, the problem was the slowness of the pace from the leaden teaching. I never liked school itself though, just hated being shut up inside all day, I much preferred being outdoors, and also liked being left to be on my own. Thus I was happiest away from school and also from home with its chores (though I learned that when I was reading a book I was pardoned and my brother got the job). Other times I would wander off to some hidden spot where I would just daydream and watch birds and other creatures. There were far more about in those days with large flocks of many, and the plumes of tens of thousands of Starlings wheeling in the sky were quite wondrous.

There were so many more lives everywhere. Crossing the meadow behind the old barn on a summer day the air was crammed with little, littler and tiniest bugs, slow and fast, huge numbers flying every direction at once. The air above full of birds wheeling and darting, scooping up the insects. The ponds and ditches were full of wee fish, mostly sticklebacks and uncountable frogs, toads and newts likewise. One friend from the next village had a damp, dank cellar where we used to go watching the newts, there were so many, we tried to arrange races but they weren't compliant and would play dead.

As I said beyond the garden and orchard in the old barn or rather barns, were redundant horse wagons and old machinery, strangely worn pieces of timber and cast iron troughs and bowls. Huge sacks of grain and animal feed were stacked high, we were told not to touch but the sugar beet pellets were often taken and chewed. We never touched the huge blocks of rock salt though, these were licked by the cattle so best avoided. The cattle were mostly fattening beef and these were housed in a part of the barns with a corrugated sheet tin walled yard where they could get some air in winter. Straw was added daily to keep their feet dry so the floor slowly rose, slowly but relentlessly until the beasts would be looking down over the wall at you.

It was here I found a plant of four-leaved clover, visions of riches, I just knew this was potentially valuable. I pulled the plant up and took it to my parents. Now it could have been easily grown on and propagated but my parents were not helpful nor green fingered for they stuck it in a bucket of water, and very soon it was rotten and thrown away. Perhaps that was my first prospect of a horticultural career. My Aunt Bertha who was a gardener was horrified when she heard my story of my loss.

Other folks' gardens

I loved flowers, and fruits, and always wanted to have a little garden of my own. My 'silly' grandma gave me not one but two places to sow the packets of seed I'd scrounged, one was between the back of a thick shrub border and the side of a bank in dark shade from a hawthorn hedge atop. Here a few weeds survived. The other was up against the bungalow wall right under the eaves, as a tall laurel hedge was within arms' length it was so shady and dry not even weeds grew there though to be fair a couple of cacti survived for nearly a year. Success was not exactly forthcoming.

Aunt Bertha was more sensible, an amateur flower gardener herself, shame we did not get to visit her so often (remember, Amy had stolen, worse then dumped, Bertha's fiancée so they had 'issues'). Auntie Bertha loved to walk to the many parks in Norwich. At the time this was a most floriferous city with beds of colourful flowers everywhere. Beds and borders in the parks, and on roundabouts and roadsides, whole regiments of them. All with a background aroma of chocolate coming from a factory by the town centre. Aunt Bertha loved flowers and showed me how she tended her small plot. Behind her house was a real old fashioned cottage garden; over-full of plants and flowers, tall rose bushes amongst even taller hollyhocks and delphiniums, little apparent order though everything weeded and neat. I especially loved the watering, what kid wouldn't, and mostly because she had a hosepipe which was just so much fun.

My first plot where even a weed might survive, indeed many did, was a small square cut in the orchard at home. This continually reverted to couch grass, nettles and horseradish in the light shade of the old apple trees. Having already learnt by abject failure the primary importance of sunlight and water I was now becoming acquainted with the problems of weed competition. None the less I grew the usual assortment of childrens' plants: sunflowers, nigella, marigolds, opium poppies... these last given me by my Nan who still grew them 'just in case' as they had old medicinal value. Her village shop had sold opium pills 'a penny's worth of comfort' and many patent medicines and other cure-alls until the late 1920s as Dickleburgh Mere, a foetid lake in the middle of the Moor caused many locals to suffer 'ague', presumably malaria.

I mentioned the shallow damp ditch on one side of the orchard had wild strawberries, almost spherical tiny red balls, barely sweet but packed full of perfume. These were my first transplanting success even surviving in the plot after all my other gems had been choked out. I'd slowly collected plants I liked, initially mostly wild flowers I'd dug while rambling, some plants even starting to survive into second years so my methods were improving.

I remember winning a prize at the Eye show for a jar of named wild flowers, and another for my jam, even one for Swiss roll, that's difficult to make but to be fair I had little competition. This was made in our new kitchen father had built in the new extension.

I guess I was seven maybe eight when we started building the new extension. Actually this is a guesstimate, my father was not exactly rapid at doing things and not earning enough, improvement was only possible thanks to Gov't grants. Which ironically he said took so long to progress and so rule laden that with our building a real toilet we had to have a proper concrete septic tank, this was finished at almost the same time the Gov't started digging up the road outside for the village to have modern mains sewage laid on making our brand new septic tank a foolish waste and expense.

Slowly our lean-to chicken shed kitchen of corrugated iron was replaced by a brick built kitchen come diner, with a pantry and a bathroom with a toilet. Although very modest these were essentially modern, the bath was wonderful with a coal fired Rayburn in the kitchen for cooking also providing a tank full of very hot water in a warming cupboard, with a lovely snug space at the bottom I could curl up in.

The old iron sheets had been pulled down then stood, leaning on the back of the rabbit hutches and dog kennels, the country way is never get rid of something in case you may need it, and don't move it far, or twice. Which soon proved the case. Although born into a forerunner of sleepy hollow we had had the seldom used wireless (radio), huge brutish thing with massive batteries and valves you could warm your hands over. Later, in the new kitchen we got the TV. Up till then life was idyllic, rural and child simple if more than a tad brutal, but with the intrusion of daily news we got paranoia, at about the worst time in history you could imagine.

In 1962 the Cuban missile crisis brought home The Cold War to many and in East Anglia we were host to a dozen or more US and UK military airbases, all prime targets. As children we only half understood how worried our parents, teachers and neighbours were. The awful reality was so close my father dug a trench in the vegetable bed and reused those handy corrugated iron sheets to cover it over then submerged those with a mound of the soil dug from the trench. It was all so traumatic, we practiced running down the garden and throwing ourselves in the trench, until it had filled with water that is. Then the prospect looked grimmer still, stay above ground and fry or get in the trench and drown. Fortunately for the world the crisis passed but I was haunted by the nuclear threat most of my life and to this day am still 'flash' aware. So much so that as late as 1982 when I came here I carefully built a reinforced 'safe refuge' under a home made elevated waterbed.

Sadly 'War' references were ubiquitous, not only the Cold War in the news but every comic and magazine seemed to be full of plucky Brits and Yanks versus ghastly Nazis, that is until ghastly Russians took their place. I remember the first book I read from the school 8-11 library, it was 'A bomb in a submarine' which I oddly imagined would be some massive bomb plunging unexploded into the ship causing all sorts of interesting engineering problems. Far from that, it was an espionage story about a spy smuggling in a wee bomb in a paper parcel, I was so disappointed. The wireless had plays and stories of military and espionage daring do and when the TV arrived that offered a similar diet though with more American input. I never much liked most 'action' stories, crime thrillers, war movies, and really loathed cowboy westerns' nearly as much as musicals -which last just seemed bizarre to me. Once on a special treat trip to the cinema, a very rare thing, mother teased the film was neither a western nor a musical. It was Oklahoma and thus both! Weirdly, as pointed out by a musical girlfriend, I sing to myself much of the time and appear to know well many of the songs from the great musicals, she wondered how and when I'd ever learned them. Perhaps I've erased those trips from my memory. I still never watch any of the above, perhaps I'm saving those for my dotage.

To be fair I do have a photo of myself in a cowboy outfit, the Lone Ranger, for the village show. I guess, probably under duress from mother who loved to be creative working on costumes. Fancy Dress was often the theme of kid's parties and the costumes would be all hand made, no such stuff for hire back then. I remember going in a dyed dark brown long armed top and clinging leggings with a specially knitted

Balaclava helmet, eye holes only like the SAS. This was bright red from throat to mouth and ash grey the rest above, with a cardboard former in the top to make it stand cylindrical- so with all this on I looked like a burning cigar! Oh so politically correct!

There was a small cinema in Diss though too expensive for us so the occasional visits were really special treats. We would pass by the front each time we visited town when we would be enthralled by the bright posters. I remember the first film I really really wanted to see- I forget the name – naturally it had a huge dinosaur on the poster. Of course it never happened. Another disappointment happened there (as did a few more later during teenage years…) when the promotional monkeys for a tea company were supposed to appear in the flesh. We queued from before dawn, easy for country folk, just stood there into the morning, on and on we waited, and then were told the event was cancelled, the monkeys were not well, I think we were fobbed off with a sample packet of tea apiece.

By this time I'd become a proto geek, a nerd, anorak, bighead or whatever epithet dullards in their incomprehension now give to the fully functional. As we were living soon after the war there remained some small respect for backroom Boffins so if your geek-dom extended into explosives, ballistics, rockets or similar tech then you were grudgingly accepted. I was adept at making things and the 'rockets' I constructed from plastic bottles surprisingly realistic. And to be fair much better than similar efforts seen on the kids' program Blue Peter. My reputation was sealed amongst the other kids though for out in the woods we made some of them fly for real powered by pilfered Guy Fawkes Night fireworks and the contents of unspent ammunition.

The dinosaur addiction which seems to grip all kids at some point joined with my natural history curiosity and then widened into other antiquities all of which fascinated me. I collected more and more old 'things' for my museum which of course became over-stocked as folk gave me/dumped stuff. Eclectic does not give the breadth, this was a completely random collection yet I found each new thing fascinating in itself.

I read insatiably and much preferred non fiction, books on making things, doing things, and of course blowing things up. I was soon into science fiction starting at the heavy end philosophically with H.G. Wells going on to the impractical but delightful Jules Verne and then the imagination and logic of Asimov. As with religion I found it hard to fuse their worlds with my reality, both seemed remote and fantastical. The contrast between my earliest years in truly archaic conditions and the impinging 'modern' world was intense. I remember being held close held close to the huge old valve wireless to listen in wonder to the beep of Sputnik passing overhead. Later I cried when I learned Laika the first dog in space would not be coming safe home, followed by a whole troop of condemned monkeys (ah perhaps that's where the tea-promotion ones went...). I realise now such tests needed to be made but back then these animals seemed so callously treated. I loved animals, they were always so friendly, warm and nuzzly, save Bob 'silly' grandmothers dog who was always chained as he was so fierce, or was so fierce as he was always chained, and quite nice if you were quiet, and fed him treats when no-one was about.

Science fiction was such a delight to me, I just loved the ideas, the new ways of thinking and the possibilities. I could read stories with visions of another world. The Eagle was a favourite comic with Dan Dare fighting the Mekon (a thinly veiled allegory) and with those strangely androgynous

Venusians. Mind you it was a blue plastic spaceman model that came in a cereal box that really transfixed me, the pair of oxygen bottles had such lovely curves top and bottom, early sexual yearnings I suppose.

Certainly growing up on a farm I had plenty of education on sexual behaviour amongst animals, it was all round, even watching a man going underneath to help the stallion enter a mare, putting the buck rabbit with the does and watching the barnyard cockerel strut his stuff. However girls were a different story, I was fascinated but in those days we were all kept apart, even with separate playgrounds at school. I had to make do with blurry photos torn from newspapers, especially the perfidious News of the World, full of human weaknesses being exploited to make sales as my grandfather and father grumbled while they avidly read it, this of course made it immediately more appealing.

These pictures I assembled along with others from magazines, mostly showing ladies in underwear, much of which somehow resembled military fortifications. Though these were a small part of an expanding collection of all sorts. I had an insatiable interest in every part of natural history, anything living or dead was collected for my museum, as I called the old chicken shed. I had trays of fossils (mainly countless ammonites and belemnites) and Roman pottery found on walks, with feathers and bones, dilapidated stuffed birds, owl pellets, rabbit skins I was trying to tan, pet cat's tails (useful for cleaning 78rpm records) and a dead weasel in a jar (never opened and surprisingly remaining intact even though not properly treated in any way, I still have this memento tucked away somewhere at the back in my current 'shed).

My musuem shed had been bought already well second hand, it was first used when we moved hens to glean each field after harvesting. It was assembled from panels and light enough to drag. When too frail to drag any more it was whitewashed and became my museum, stood next to the dog kennels. Later when we sold the farm the shed came to Dickleburgh where it housed Granddad's lawnmower and garden tools. I moved it again when I arrived here in '82 using it to screen the neighbours until the hedge I planted grew up, when it was moved to it's current and likely final resting place in the orchard, as a henhouse once again.

As our house was small so this shed provided extra room and kept me safely out of the way, for although we were a country family, my collections were a bit macabre even for them, or maybe just plain smelly, especially my attempts to cure skins and furs and stuff critters for display. Not so much taxidermy as arrested decomposition in many cases. And as the shed was even damper than the house even the once properly prepared stuffed fox I'd been donated soon gave off whiffy waves of decay.

Owl pellets were fascinating, I collected these small woolly sausages from under the owls' perching places. By soaking with soapy water these broke up, softening the mix further with soda you could pick out a multitude of tiny bones and bleach those. Then I tried to work out what the owl had eaten; a bird or rodent, and assemble the bones in some semblance on cards. This process was not all that pongy unlike some of my tanning experiments. Over a few years my efforts at taxidermy improved but slightly and most of my best efforts slowly developed forms of life after death each contributing its own unique aroma. Perhaps the less said about my extensive dung & droppings collection the better (and I have yet to find a mole dropping, as apparently has anyone else, my theory was they smear it on the sides of their runs to attract food, I dug many runs to see if they construct part as a mole-latrine, never managing to find one).

I was really interested in anything mechanical, and with 'inventing' new things, most were totally impossible or impractical of course, and if ever then badly built- mostly because of the foolish tools allowed for kids to use. Barred from using the proper tools (quite rightly, these were few and valuable) we were often given safer, ie blunt, copies that could not do the job. So naturally any wood tougher than Balsa was too hard to saw, shaping any metal thicker than old biscuit tin was near impossible and nails always trumped screws. (Likewise in the garden, I was given a toy trowel, it bent into a U the first time I tried to dig a hole and an old hoe so round edged you could not have cut a cake let alone a weed, whereas on the farm the hoes' were sharp as razors.) Thus the tool of choice/necessity too frequently resorted to was a hammer. It is amazing what one of these can do if administered with enthusiasm. Putting things back together after though…

Still, the challenge of building things was the more rewarding, probably as you could 'show these off' and gain kudos. Beginning with traditional go carts of course though these were hard work to move as everywhere was so flat. I made all sorts of contrivances, with string and bells to warn me of approaching strangers… Even set up tin-cans-on-a-string walky talky to my brother in the barn, surprisingly this last did work, mainly because twas not mine own invention as I'd copied one I'd seen.

Rather presciently I spent a lot of effort trying to make my own laser using quartz crystals, a hollow glass tube from ye olde truck battery and a flashlight. Fortunately this failed to cut down trees, or do anything except perturb my family even more who were now sure I was more than a bit odd. I'd started with dismantling toys, and clocks and then all sorts of broken stuff was given to me that 'would keep me quiet'. Keep me quiet, true, and I accumulated even more sorts of odd things, and acquired quite a skill in taking things apart. Which eventually became the skill of putting things back together and even making things work. I still take great pleasure in 'fixing' and making things work, especially in radical ways. Why buy anew or fix it the 'right' way with expensive parts if you suspect there's another, probably less costly, option/bodge?

It was in my 'museum' I did my chemical experiments, mostly failing-to-make: fireworks, potions, poisons, and drugs, more witchcraft and wizardry than science. Inspired by the Sunday newspapers lurid tales of debauchery and untold riches awaiting I was taken by the idea of becoming the local Opium farmer. Fortunately thwarted as I had no idea how to actually grow and process the plants, nor any conception of the huge area, sheer number of plants and the labour required, and anyway my Nan who had given me the poppies to grow had not grown or rather not given me the right sort. She'd told how she sold Opium pills against the Ague fever when she was young and that when used as medicine or to help sleep 'they never did no-one no harm' as she put it. So she believed at the time, and neither did those Copper and Boron salts she included with her pickles and bottled fruit. On the other hand she was 'agin' the use of anything as a drug, even tobacco for women, back then smoking was promoted as 'manly' and not harmful, though the 'wrong' thing for a woman to do showing 'loose' ways. My unusual interest in so many areas along with just reading so many books got me the nickname of 'Prof'. I guess this sort of showed respect from some kids though it encouraged worse bullying from the dimmer ones who feared anyone with 'learning'. Many years later I was chatting with an ex-con and expressed my worst fear of being imprisoned was the bullying and violence this would apparently bring. He assured me all I had to do was let it be known how much I as a gardener knew of poisons as he reckoned that would be a most powerful form of protection for apparently poisoners are much feared by the ignorant! Also, being well versed in brewing and fermentation methods could bring added benefits and protection from the 'bosses'. Fortunately I have never needed his advice. Although looking back I see how my early years were hardly idyllic they were not as now. The lack of the modern parental panic did give us children an independence few can enjoy today. We were left to our own interests and allowed to go where we wanted pretty much unsupervised from very young. Then cycling was seen as good exercise and not dangerous for the roads were then so quiet. In fact territorial dogs chasing you was a much more likely hazard. From early on I rode my old maroon bicycle for miles around, most often on my own. This bike was another point of friction with my brother who, growing larger, had been bought a nearly new modern bicycle with cable brakes and lights while I was fobbed off with an old, near antique, boneshaker. Still it was freedom to go where and when as I wanted.

I remember one hot summer day having strayed a little far and being dreadfully thirsty stopping by a village pump on a common in a village I barely knew. Now I had experience of a hand-pump as since tiny I had watched my mother use the village pump to bring up water from a well near the church (presumably no-one ever thought of the seepage from the graveyard...). I worked this pump and cool water issued, I drank greedily, never for a moment considering any possible connection with the greened over duck pond only a few yards away! A day later I was heaving at both ends and was very ill for weeks, of course in those days a pond was the receptacle for all sorts of village effluent!

Mind you, occasional trips to the seaside were not much better. I remember first time rushing into the sea (I've never had any fear of water and had learned to swim early on when an aunt had taken me to a pool in Norwich, which treat I then demanded whenever possible, my favourite exercise, still). Anyway I was splashing around in the sea when I noticed these brown sausages about me- need I say more! That resulted in another bout of sickness and a strange ailment that persisted. At the time it went undiagnosed but describing this to a doctor when I was a student he considered I may well have contracted a mild case of Polio, however he also reckoned I had been fortunate as if this had been diagnosed at the time I would have been treated and this could have led to a far worse outcome.

In some ways I probably benefitted from these sicknesses and the so many infectious diseases that went the rounds for as the old saying goes 'that which does not kill me only makes me stronger' as I have enjoyed a superbly functioning immune system ever since. My rate of healing after accidents seldom failed to surprise.

However I've always suffered from the cold which soon makes me poorly, I just do not stay warm enough on my own unless moving vigorously around. At night I get colder and colder, without the hot water bottles and cats I reckon I would never have made it as a child. School as I noted was not too bad in this one respect, home was much colder, and farm chores were miserably done in the open, or not much warmer in a freezing shed or barn.

The big freeze
Through the colder months we normally endured the conditions, doing what we could and this usually by simply wearing more layers of clothes. (The old habit of 'bundling',

sewing children into their winter clothes, was still in living memory, and I'm not sure wasn't still being done by some at Primary school.) But most cold winters were as nothing compared to the extreme weather during the winter of '62/'63. We enjoyed a white Christmas despite the cold which got worse, and worse as the new year progressed, week after week after month after month of snow and cold, huge icicles hanging everything. No water, no power, no cars or transport for days on end. Well it was much worse than we had been used to before so we just had to huddle closer to the fire. It was hard on the animals though, we lost many, they could not eat frozen food and water, the wildlife fared worse, I remember dead birds littering the hedge banks like fallen leaves.

The unusual cold meant all sorts of strange events were taking place with tree trunks exploding and beer frozen in barrels in cellars. We heard Diss mere had frozen so hard that they'd driven a tractor across. Dickleburgh moor flooded and froze over, luckily we were able to get there and see folk ice skating, my brother and I were pulled along on an ice sled. So once home again my brother and I tried to do the same with home-made sleds of wooden crates and slid these about on the ice on our farm pond. Somehow we survived.

One day we came close to ruining the family. Of necessity my brother had been entrusted to my care from early on, a risky venture that usually worked out okay. However after school one day I'd caught a chill and was forced to go to bed leaving him to run feral. Shortly he was screaming from down in the garden below that the barn was on fire. I stuck my head out and oh my god it was. By then we had a telephone so I rang 999, and by chance this was picked up by my mother working as telephonist at the time. She barely believed me thinking it was some sort of practical joke I'd made up. It was too late anyway, the stockyard barn was timber and thatch, as old and dry as it could get. By the time the fire engine arrived many cattle were dead or had to be put down and we lost a favourite cat who went back in to rescue her kittens just before the roof fell. On investigating the ruins the firemen discovered cigarette butts and used matches. Odd as my brother had surely been too young to try smoking, I'd not seen him try by then, but then no-one else was or had been around. The conclusion was obvious yet he pleaded innocence and this small disaster remained unsolved.

I was lucky, or fortunate, as I was often a tad reckless and sustained quite a few mishaps, most of which I tried to keep secret. One time making rockets from old ammunition I had one fly off the washing line (trying to make it skoot along held by runners) and struck me on the hand, I still have an ache in that little finger, presumably a break as the pain was intense and persisted for months. Ironically this was my writing hand and made most school work extremely difficult. I

did not think clearly and used father's camera to take some photos of some of those experiments, which he of course saw as soon as the film was developed, was in deep trouble for that.

Later at secondary school I had an accident pushing a glass tube into a stopper in science class, this severed a tendon so my right index finger is permanently stiff and turned down at the last joint. Of course there was no sympathy, enquiry or even first aid, I was told off for being stupid and made to continue with a handkerchief wrapped around. Now I guess such an accident would probably result in investigation and probably compensation, back then it was considered your own fault. With both injuries persisting through life I still find writing and precise manipulation difficult, ironically not a good start for authoring and gardening careers!)

Holidays?
From financial limitations even though both my parents worked and because a mixed farm is hard to leave we never took holidays and rarely a family trip out, even visits to the seaside, only twenty odd miles away, were infrequent. Actually a blessing as in those days as I told earlier how the sea was so vilely polluted, I noted my first and only swim from the beach at Great Yarmouth was cut short when we realised I was in a stew of turds and worse. Indeed I just did not realise how beautiful a sea could be till I got to travel abroad, for to me as a child, and still, our sea was browny grey, oily, filthy and smelt like a sewer; the North Sea, known in French as la Mer du Nord, pronounced Merde du Nord.
Fortunately on stays with either Aunt Bertha or 'silly' grandmother I might get visits to the swimming pool or Lido to really swim, and always enjoyed the parks which had bathing places. Norwich had so many parks and these were very well maintained and full of flowers back then. I loved to wander along looking at the long borders and remember preferring the scented flowers, and still do.
I also loved the museums, for Norwich had many. It was fascinating seeing curious relics of times past and I could spend all day browsing though my brother usually bored quickly so we often left rather too soon for me. He was also bored on car trips which I did not mind loving the changing vista of hedge and verge and the fields beyond. Much of East Anglia is flattish with the trees thinly spread and this gives the illusion of you being about to enter a forest, you just never get there. But look at those hedges and verges, the

variety and interest is huge, of course it was even better back then.

One memorable trip was to Moyes Hall in Bury St Edmunds where we were transfixed by the most macabre exhibits. Old coffins, medical instruments, a wooden bicycle and a lock of Napoleons' hair were really interesting. Wow, it was the death mask of Corder the infamous Red Barn murderer that thrilled, and beside was a book bound in his very own leather like skin! We often demanded to be taken back there.

Ipswich museum was larger though less inspiring save it had a monstrous piece of amber the size of half a brick. This semi-precious fossilised tree resin is allegedly washed up on East Anglian beaches and on EVERY visit for near seventy years I have searched for some. Aunt Bertha once gave me a piece to help. Sadly this was Cornelian not Amber so never helped my quest though I have a whole bowl full of near misses which are rather predictably mostly Cornelians with some Garnets and quartz and not even one tiny piece of Amber despite my having searched countless miles of beach so often. I even took a sack of salt and a tin bath down to Dunwich, made up a strong salty solution with sea water and shovelled the gravel through. The idea was the Amber would float, nothing did. Got a lot of interest from the fishermen who thought I was after bait.

Then I made a discovery, a UV torch sold for disclosing dog pee makes Amber fluoresce. At night you can see a piece from a distance and pick a gem out from a beach full of gravel, as I practised with a genuine piece. Eventually after a large number of nocturnal trips I have examined much if not most of the Norfolk and Suffolk coastline and still found none. There really is very little washed up most of the time! Seems some may be there, but about as common as meteorites.

Possibly the most evocative of all places was Grimes Graves near Thetford. East Anglia has no stone worth mentioning, the biggest rocks we have are flint nodules which now have little use other than for making decorative patterns in brick walls. Any worked stone you see, say on the corners of church walls, is imported from far away. But in prehistoric times flint was THE tool as freshly broken it has edges as sharp as glass. Grimes Graves are stone age mines older than the pyramids, they dug deep pits down into the chalk to find the flint as it is most workable when fresh dug. Some of these mines had been re-excavated and to climb down a steep deep rickety ladder to the bottom was as exciting as any safari. You could stare at intestinal tunnels covered in tool marks and holes made thousands of years in the past looking as if the miners had only just left. This amazing place has had the same lasting impression on my children who also consider this the most interesting place they ever visited.

There is an odd thing about childhood, as I remember it all seems now to be not so much my colourful personal history but a more distant black and white past from even longer ago. I guess this is what happens when you look back from over seven decades!

The new old school
At eleven having successfully appealed my failed 11 plus I moved to Eye Grammar School while everyone else went to the Secondary Modern leaving me bereft of friends for few from Primary school would ever speak with me again. I daily had to cycle a longer way round to avoid the sneers and stones of my erstwhile school mates. Which would have been more endurable if I had indeed gone to some superior

and preferable place, but ironically that was not what I found.

Eye Grammar was antique, a Gormenghast come Hogwarts set in Sleepy Hollow. An archaic relic of public school malpractices, set in a decaying structure with doddering staff hanging on for just one more year. For as I arrived it was already closing. I was to suffer that last year of this school before we moved to another in Diss. Thus the extremely run-down condition and worn out staff. Many teachers had taught my father before me, no bad thing in itself but as with so much else making them inevitably more than a tad behind the latest knowledge. For example I remember studying 'Oil' in geography, when tested where it was to be found I included the possibility it might be found locally. To humiliating rebuke and disdain from the teacher, who had obviously not read the newspaper article I had on the latest discovery of oil in the North Sea- but a few miles distant, he was vitriolic over my importunity and lack of respect for his knowledge!

The oldest school buildings pre-dated the Armada, as did much of Eye itself, made more surreal by a Spanish Armada helmet on display in the massive church glowering over the school. Some of the buildings were mullion windowed, of wood beams, red brick and plaster as were most houses in the area. The slightly less antiquated school buildings were modelled on the Dickensian workhouse pattern. Prison-like these seemed designed to intimidate and chill, both mentally and physically as here the heating was inadequate and temperamental. Most if not all these buildings had deteriorated to very poor conditions, riddled with asbestos and rot, wiring and plumbing falling to pieces. With long broken and worn out equipment, indeed each and every desk and chair, fixture and fitting was in precisely the sort of condition one would have expected with the prospect of it all going on a bonfire the following year. In some rooms in the back row (somewhere I now fortunately avoided) the backs of the chairs had scraped grooves in the asbestos sheet panelling showering a dust underneath. This was aggravated by some 'back-rowers' scraping peepholes to the class next door.

Eye Grammar school had recently become, under some duress one suspects, a mixed school. Girls were now admitted though segregated all the time including during lessons being confined to one side of the room. The exercise yards for break were also divided into two deeply shady pits hedged about by tall austere buildings and divided by a forbidding wall. This most explicitly made the point keeping the girls safely away from us boys. The church towered overhead to one side reminding us where the power rested while looming malevolently over all was the grey flint edifice of Eye castle rising high above us on it's castle mound. A truly cinematic backdrop. This is now accessible and an excellent vantage point with steep paved near endless steps. A hard climb none the less but so much less imposing than when we clambered up through the endless scrub on the sides as we had done back then.

Each morning I would cycle down to Eye with the castle like a beacon nestling in the hollow in front while pedalling furiously to keep ahead of pursuing pupils now at the other school. As I came past their school entrance I would go full pelt to avoid yet more jibes and mud slinging. Once I'd reached the bottom of the hill there was a serpentine wall (an odd form of wall with huge curves making multiple semi-circular bays on either side so resembling a giant red brick snake) I was safe in the town with near empty narrow streets between the medieval and Tudor buildings. A gentle ride led me on to the school with a baker's shop yards before I arrived where I could buy really-fresh just-baked rolls if I had some pennies, delicious.

My first day was traumatic. We new kids were abused by the older boys, pushed, pulled, our caps thrown over walls and our heads pushed down into toilets. The teachers took no notice of the mayhem yet never failing to tell us off for being dishevelled and out of uniform. The lessons were a relief, until break when the bullying continued. We were lined up and interrogated as to whether we supported Ipswich or Norwich football team, either answer resulting in pain from the alternate supporters. As I had a total lack of interest in any team in any sport I replied so, thus inviting the ire of both.

Things did not improve thereafter. 'Chippie's Bike' was the boilers' coal shed, you would be shut in there thus missing lessons and so being punished for so doing. 'Visiting the Vicar's garden' was being dragged on top of the flat roof of the physics lab, having your trousers removed then being thrown down into the stinging nettles of the overgrown burial plot below. Another torture was 'the Garden of Eden', the toilet block, it was best to avoid this anyway as it was even less supervised than everywhere else, a lot of nasty things happened in there. It was divided by partitions and one of the older pupils' favourite past times was to make us new meat clamber over this assault course whilst being pelted with disgusting missiles and prodded with sticks.

I have a vague memory come nightmare of visiting another school for some reason and using the toilets there at break. Each toilet was a bottomless one over a channel half full of watery sludge moving downhill, faster when being filled by many bladders. Some older kids tried to float burning balls of paper under you though this luckily failed. Nasty but I must give them points for ingenuity though.

I was so relieved when I discovered the library upstairs in the oldest part of the school. This was rarely visited by the bullies and jocks and so became my safe place. It was also high up and so warm, with sun streaming through the mullions onto the shelves of fascinating tomes. I also learned that if I was forced to miss lessons because of some mishap I could slink off to and be discovered in the library reading a book... Even the worst teachers found it hard to punish me for that.

The school ethos was very old school, obedience was obligatory, dissension not allowed. Discipline was enforced as at primary school with projectiles of stubs of chalk, or worse the board rubber and ultimately the cane. And each was inflicted brutally. Just recently I re-encountered a lady who as a girl in my class I had witnessed having a wooden yard rule (3 feet, not quite a metre) broken over her head by a massive slap from an angry teacher. She said although excruciatingly painful she'd been saved by her hair band which had helped cushion the blow. Oh those good old days were not really so good were they?

Previously as I said I had had little interest in sport, or exercise, after all I was cycling several miles each day as well as a wagon load of farm and home chores. This lack of enthusiasm was then reinforced by the combination of 'sporty jock kids' and 'sporty' teachers. These had an unholy alliance against any child lacking physical prowess or worse, showing an iota of artistic or scientific interest. (And this was a Grammar school, the other, Secondary Modern, was apparently even more anti-any-learning).

A further problem, then and now, was how this alpha male brigade assumed that not only must you want to love sport as much as they, but also that everyone knew instinctively how to play each game, for the rules and tactics were still not explained to me, not once, not ever. And when I looked for books in the library on sports other than biographies there were none, how were you to learn?

What was even worse was where and how school sport was inflicted. The school's playing field was on top of a windy bald hill a long jog away. Even longer as we the most junior were lumbered with carrying everything required including the kit of all the older boys. All in full school uniform mind you, with your cap on as long as you managed to retain it. Once we got up there the changing room was a wooden pavilion with no power or washing facilities, we played under protest, dismally, in the mud, before changing back into school uniform and making the return journey.

You may note the lack of a shower, well one was possible but only back down at the main site. So changing out of our now soiled uniforms we showered, when there was time, but usually had to miss it anyway as all the larger lads took precedence. And you certainly did not risk venturing into the shower amongst them!

The trip to the playing field was sometimes okay though for on occasions when a school team was playing away we non-sporties were conveniently left behind under the supervision of any teacher willing to freeze with us, and who went ahead to open up. Thus we sauntered on the way, first amongst the tombstones in the churchyard looking for coins and gold rings (we'd heard moles could bring these up), then under Dove bridge where we tried to catch the sticklebacks in our cupped hands. We'd climb over the old gun emplacement with it's shiny stainless steel stub projecting from the massive concrete plinth and then slowly crawl the lane uphill in cool shade from long uncut hedges until we emerged into the never ending windiness of the playing field positioned like a bald patch on top a head. After the minimal time had passed we'd be let go back down again, and those times we could grab a hot shower unmolested as the sporties were away. Showering was a real treat to me as this was a new experience, and a warm one, we had only had a tin bath in the sink at first then later a proper bath at home but never a shower. It was a shame the showers were so often too risky because of the bullying and sexual harassment from the low browed, it was another place I could warm up.

The school lunch here was yet another area fraught with frustration. British school dinners were legendary in their boiled out overcooked blandness especially at schools as traditional as Eye but at least here the portions were generous. Probably this was as the sporties / jocks had huge appetites. Eaten at long tables the serving dishes were passed down with each lad taking his share until the dregs reached us newcomers. Thus we got plenty of the less palatable fare and very little of anything tasty. A lesson we already knew well, life is so not fair. You get what you can grab and hold onto and seldom what you deserve or are entitled.

The afternoon lessons would finish followed by detention for all the usual sins: being out of uniform, being dishevelled, missing lessons, talking back et al. Then it was the cycle ride home, uphill all the way. One small advantage of detention was at least I could then go by the direct route as the other school had finished earlier so there was less risk there. If I was not detained I had to pass that school just as everyone hung about outside, so then it was wiser to go the long, long way round.

One of the measures I soon learned to take was to keep my bicycle pump and lights in my satchel for safe-keeping and also to take out my tyre valves and keep these in my pocket or I would find them gone and have to push the bike home. Oh those ********. And reporting such theft to the teachers just got you in trouble as "that sort of thing doesn't happen here boy, stop making up stories and wasting my time!" Were there any good moments? Well the science club was right up my alley, we were allowed to do all sorts of hands on experiments. Working with lethal chemicals and dangerous reactions was fun! As I said, Health & Safety was not then much of an issue. Thank you Mr Parker for keeping my curiosity alive. And for helping me find how to make the most amazing bangs from all sorts of mixtures. I remember using a couple of then fairly common household products (which I best not name) painted as a solution which when dried exploded at the slightest touch. Such were the days… That year was surprisingly one of my happier in some ways, my bother, sorry brother, was still at junior school and I was on my own more of the time free to ride further on my bicycle. I travelled the lanes and byways in ever increasing circles until I had exhausted every place of interest. As I had done earlier much of my interest was poking about in derelict places and quietly sitting in some hidden place watching critters come and go, sometimes setting traps for them. One of my crazier ideas was making a landmine from cordite extracted from the unexploded ordnance, this packed into a tin ignited by a hot wire from a battery when a bunny or pheasant walked over a tinfoil switch. It presumably scared the shit out of some poor animal though I never found anything to cook. As interesting as this was the result was poor return for the effort so I went back to snares. I saved the remaining propellant for my other forbidden fruit of rockets which I continued experimenting with until the boxes of ammo ran out. Then I was obliged to work out how to make my own fuel from weed killer, fertiliser and paper pulp, this was safe enough wet but when dry was rather unstable. Once while drying a quite small amount for touch-paper I blew the Rayburn oven door off. My poor mother, from the day it was installed I had had a series of 'accidents' with this wonderful device. An early cracker was my lifting the pressure cooker valve whilst it was boiling blackberries, the superheated burst of purple slush gave our brand new kitchen a unique, enduring and rather in-fashion tie-die effect.

Other than ruining that batch, and the décor, I was good at jam and jelly making, it was like experimenting, and it involved large quantities of fruit and SUGAR. I adore both of these and can never get enough of either. Thus I ate as much as I made, and often afterwards with a serious sugar buzz I'd rush off on some ostensible errand to disappear into the fields or off on my bike for a while.

As mentioned before, there was a general run-down aspect to most places. In all the surrounding villages stood many half forgotten sheds and empty buildings, the folk had moved elsewhere or were lost in the wars. Many houses especially the largest were standing abandoned as the costs of repair outran their value. These were all exciting places to poke in, though dangerous as many were in the process of falling down. Near Redgrave Fen, the source of the Waveney, one hall had all but disappeared leaving the remains of an Italian prisoner of war camp and a Victorian cupola observatory most oddly situated in the dense woods. Deep within those woods was a large stone statue of Cerberus the three headed dog from the Classics (and oddly employed on the label of tins of salt). What a grotesque object to find apparently dropped at random into an English scene.

Another advantage of cycling was I could spend even more time at Dickleburgh with my grandfather Alf who was always up to something interesting. Instead of trying to persuade my mother to take me I could cycle over in half an hour.

Alf liked to be out at night in the dark, many of his pursuits required this and I liked it too, not finding it frightening nor scary, and full of interesting smells and goings on. As he said "nothing in the dark will hurt you that ain't also going to hurt in the light". At home I could seldom sneak out at night as I had to pass through my parents' room so visiting Grandad Alf was welcome opportunity to do so. When he could we would go fishing followed by the trip at dawn or 'sparrow 'fart' as he termed it to the railway station to collect the daily newspapers and sundries for the shop. One night he taught me to pick ripe strawberries, (and other fruits) by moonlight. You cannot see red by moonlight but you can see greeny white unripe fruits, you feel for the truss, feel for a fruit you can touch but not see, it must be red and thus ripe. (Beware, dark slugs in holes in ripe fruits are also invisible...)

Anyway as I had become of an age where I could be quiet (well almost) and pay attention so I was allowed to stay over more often and accompany Alf to the local Workers Educational Association meetings. These were lectures, often with slideshows, many on natural history. I was technically too young to attend but who was bothered if I was interested, and kept quiet.

Although occasionally going over my head I was transfixed by the talks and fascinated by some of the exhibits. Such talks on archaeology, history, local history and especially those on wildlife were all eagerly anticipated for days before and then so enjoyed.

One I've often remembered was a chap who back from the Far East had a slide show of the places he'd been, and amongst many curious souvenirs had brought an unusual delicacy, a bit of stick with what seemed like dried grapes stuck on- much later I learned a piece of Hovenia dulcis, the Japanese Raisin tree. I was hooked, what fascinatingly strange fruits were to be found in the World. That one event left me with insatiable curiosity. Few fresh fruits other than those grown locally were available in rural nineteen sixties. A real 'treat' was a tinned pineapple ring or peach slice with custard. Oranges and bananas were but seldom seen and as with dried dates at Christmas were considered exotic.

(As so many kids I tried to grow the seeds from the new fruits I came across, most of which failed, not surprisingly. However my methods slowly improved with the decades and since coming back to Dickleburgh I've grown a Raisin tree from seed, which has since fruited, so one life long mission completed.)

After the evening talks he would stop round his friend, the butchers (where his lurchers were kept) for a drink and cards. As I said these were much more commonly played back then. I got pretty good at Rummy, Pontoon (Blackjack or 21), and Cribbage, but of course could never beat the old boys. I still love Cribbage, the mathematical precision, the scoring by rote and moving the pegs along the board, the neatness of it, such a clever game.

After we'd walk his dogs in the dark, up the street, round through the allotments, along the fields by the stream and back through the churchyard staying well away from home in case Nan caught sight of us and found he'd not got rid of the dogs, again.

One very late night as we snuck in the back door the church clock rang repeated by the clock on the hall table. Nan came from the bedroom wide eyed and determined. "I told you to get rid of those dogs, I know you were out with them again just now..." He had to comply but seemed broken by this.

In those years after he gave up the dogs so did his vigour, his country walks, night time trips and even days at the races palled. As with so many others he turned on the TV, tuned in and dropped off. After Nan passed away he got dogs again though seldom did he venture out anywhere much, after all he had now become a pensioner, and his old wounds were grinding him down.

And anyway why go? The hunting had become poorer, riskier and unprofitable. In only a few years the rabbits were all myxied, the hares few, and runoff into the rivers and meres had poisoned their fish. Worse you would soon be spotted, the countryside was no longer empty, peaceful nor quiet anymore. There were cars and trucks, day and night, close by and heard in the distance. With suddenly unexpectedly and too often the peaceful sky shattered by jet aircraft roaring past to chase those pesky Russians away. For the older rustic world I'd been dropped into and glimpsed had long been dying away, the new behemoth had arrived; noise, motion and plastic supplanting everything. The country was gripped 'in the white heat of technology'. Kennedy announced we were going to the moon and on the wireless (now called Radio and soon 'Tranny' or transistor radio) the Beatles and Rolling Stones were ushering in a psychedelic age with such exciting sounding sins as sex, drugs and rock & roll, and that was, well, interesting...

I stood there on the edge of puberty about to move to my new school in Diss, gazing forwards, evidently into another world. Realising, to paraphrase L. P. Hartley in the Go-between, that "the future is also a foreign country, they'll do things differently there".

a family history

The surname Flowerdew and variations is thought to have originated as Fleure de Dieu, Flower of God, probably the blue Flax flower known to Flemish linen weavers, or it may have been a corruption of Fleur de Lys, the Lily of French royalty.
Earliest recorded are John Flowerdew /Flowerdue who was instituted to the rectory of Drayton near Norwich, Norfolk on the 15th of March, 1461 and a William Flowerdew 1470-1536 living at Wymondham.
The clan continued as part of the farming community in South Norfolk and North Suffolk (known as the Waveney valley) and although never numerous slowly spread to the furthest reaches of the globe with Flowerdews among the very first settlers or 'Ancient Planters' of what is now the USA, see below.

Notable Flowerdews
Flowerdews infest every continent, apparently including such remote places as Tierra del Fuego. One Flowerdew, founder of the famous Hethersett tea plantation (said to be the most valuable tea at the time) in Sri Lanka (then Ceylon), is buried under the main runway of the Seychelles airport.

Freddie Flowerdew was a famous popular music composer in the period before the Second World War, his tunes are played on a piano in an episode of the TV Jeeves and Wooster series. Freddie's name also appears on a theatre front in the backdrop of a scene from a Woody Allen film.

During the late nineteen sixties one Arthur? Flowerdew became momentarily famous by having 'odd' dreams, these resulted in him being taken to Petra for a documentary by the BBC where he revealed otherwise unknowable evidence suggesting re-incarnation.

A braver than average Flowerdew, Gordon, from Billingford, the next village but one to mine, won a V.C. in the First World War. The family story is he and his brother had gone to market, sold not only the corn, but also the horses and wagons and run off to Canada. Later they joined up to lead an important part in the campaign, their fatal charge has been portrayed by the painter Munnings, another and even more famous local.

Tendency to write

At the present day amongst the few hundred members of the clan are remarkably many in the arts and sciences, with as well as myself a statistically impressive number of published authors, both of fiction and non fiction:

P. Flowerdew, Phyllis Flowerdew, Douglas Flowerdew, Lynne Flowerdew, Robin Flowerdew, John Flowerdew, Jennifer Flowerdew, Dorothy W. Flowerdew, J. R. Flowerdew, and A. D. J. Flowerdew. Herbert Flowerdew was Victorian author of 'The woman's view', a novel about marriage, and 'The Celibate's wife', beyond belief these'd be publishable now-a-days.

The Kett Rebellion
In the sixteenth century Flowerdews were involved with, or to be fair caused, the Kett Rebellion against enclosure. Peasants were angry and desperate as all over the country the common lands were (legally in the strictest sense but wrongly) stolen and enclosed to feed flocks of sheep for the expanding wool industry. In the summer of 1549 the rebellion was sparked off by a turf war over land between Hethersett and Wymondham being enclosed by both Robert Kett and his neighbour bastion of the local gentry, Serjeant John Flowerdew, Steward to the Duke of Norfolk. Allegedly each alternately paying local drunks and malcontents to level the other's hedges and fences. Flowerdew was already rather unpopular being 'the establishment' and was libelled as having pocketed the Lead from dissolving the abbey at Wymondham, which he had over-seen under Henry VIII.

Kett assembled a small band under "Kett's Oak' still standing on the old Norwich road just outside Wymondham. More joined and the rebellion escalated, and while Flowerdew legged it to call the authorities Kett's followers began a general mayhem which led to the eponymous peasant revolt with many (est. 16K+) thousands of the poor and dispossessed capturing the nearby city of Norwich. Kett made a declaration of human rights, political and religious reform and demanded justice. This is little known but without much doubt is the original inspiration for the later American declarations, his great granddaughter Temperence being one of the first Jamestown settlers arriving on the Falcon in 1609, see below.

Unfortunately the King's advisors were not minded to settle things with reason and justice but to impose their power with force, which unfortunately the rebellion gave cause.

While they camped on Mousehold Heath, a hill overlooking the city of Norwich (then the 2nd or 3rd biggest city in Britain), the worst members started to party, then rob and riot for provisions. They drank the city dry and are said to have barbecued 20,000 of their woolly enemies before they were betrayed with false promises then set upon with outright warfare by an army led by the Earl of Warwick. 3,000 were slaughtered, more executed with Kett hung from the castle battlements and the rest brutally disbanded.

The unofficial longstanding Flowerdew motto of "better hang for the flock than the lamb" appears to have originated from that time.

One of John Flowerdew's (seven sons!) daughter in laws was Frances Appleyard daughter of Roger Appleyard son of Sir Nicholas Appleyard of Bracon Ash b.1482 d.1511 while SIMULTANEOUSLY Robert Kett was married to Alice Appleyard b/ c.1493 d 1549 another daughter of Sir Nicholas A. Thus this infamous rebellion may have started more as a family squabble!

Strange death of Amy Robsart / Anne Dudley

Flowerdews were also rumoured to be involved in the peculiar demise of Amy Robsart / Amy/Anne Dudley, b.1532-d.1560 (said to have been pushed down the stairs in her house at Cumnor) she being the (inconvenient) wife of Lord Leicester, he was thought to wish her gone so he could marry Queen Elizabeth I (this was novelised by Walter Scott in 'Kenilworth'). John Flowerdew, it seems that same John that started the Kett Rebellion, was her steward (Ipswich Museum has a copy of a letter to he from her regarding some sheep) so he had access as well as a family connection therefore perhaps this event was not unconnected with the closely following rise of one of his sons, Edward (Member of

Parliament and judge) to the rank of Baron of the Exchequer a couple of years after.

Curiously Amy Robsart / Anne Dudley was half sister to that same John F.'s daughter in law Frances Appleyard and first lived with Lord Leicester /Dudley at Stanfield Hall near Wymondham This hall was owned by the Appleyards and then was sold to the same Edward Flowerdew in 1566 so yet again this also appears to have been another family affair.

Taking the roof off the Abbey

Also allegedly twice so far, Flowerdews have purloined the lead from off Wymondham Abbey roof. The first time was during the dissolution when some Lead (leaving the church covered) was legitimately taken for the Crown, instead it was 'accidentally' all removed then allegedly disappearing.

Later during the Civil war the Lead was stripped off the roof again, ostensibly this time to be made into bullets, and allegedly again mysteriously 'liberated'. The inevitable retributions resulted in several macabre clandestine bonfires there now being a dearth of Flowerdew bodies in graves thereabouts and even gravestones were removed though records are still held in some parishes. This may have possibly been some encouragement for our family tendency to flee abroad.

Curiously last century a large quantity of Lead was found, about a ton in one ingot, under the floor of Wymondham Abbey Chapter House during repairs. This indicates the actual thieves must have died before this valuable bounty could be retrieved, thus pointing the finger away from Flowerdews who of course survived Kett's rebellion.

Ancient Planters, founders of the USA

One of the very first settlers in North America at Jamestown well before the more famous Mayflower was Temperance Flowerdew b.1587-d.1628. She was a daughter of Anthony Flowerdew d.1610 of Hethersett and Martha Garrett/Stanley of Scottow, he son of William Flowerdew b.1530-d.1600 and Frances Appleyard. William was son of that same John Flowerdew again b.1530-d.1565 and Kate Shears also of Hethersett, the son of William Flowerdew b.1470-d.1536 and Katherine Hall of Wymondham.

Temperence Flowerdew was both great granddaughter of John Flowerdew who 'caused' the Kett Rebellion while her grandmother's father's sister, Great Aunt, was Alice the wife of Robert Kett. At the same period her grandmother's half sister was The Amy Robsart mentioned above who was allegedly murdered by her husband Robert Dudley, Earl of Leicester who'd wished to marry Elizabeth I.

With family history like that no wonder she emigrated to help found a new society!
Anyway Temperance was one of the very first settlers in North America arriving at Jamestown on the Falcon in May 1609 a few months before they commenced the 'Starving Time'. (Surviving this should have been origination for their celebration of Thanksgiving which evolved later with the following wave of settlers in the Mayflower.)
It is family legend that it was Temperance who was behind the settlements' philosophy, she & founding fathers resulting in the famous U.S. declarations of rights.
Temperance being one of the few dozen survivors of those early years remarrying wisely became, temporarily, the richest woman in America.
Much more information is coming from the 'Flowerdew Hundred' archaeological dig near Jamestown in Virginia USA. This was good tobacco land apparently as Stanley Flowerdew took a large quantity back to England in 1619. Bizarrely there's a Flowerdew Polka originating from there.

Most coincidentally when I hitch-hiked across the USA in 1978 one of the first places I was taken to see was the 'Old Customs House' near Williamsburg / Jamestown, one of the oldest US buildings, I was visiting friends, of course then I was young and knew nothing of my family's historical association. I remember us making sand candles on the beach, ironically almost on top of the original settlement.

My personal family tree

I am son of Richard John Flowerdew a farmer of Yaxley, b.1927, who m.1951 Pamela Lockett of Dickleburgh b.1929

☐

My grandfather was Robert George Flowerdew, farmer, of Yaxley b.1879 d.1952 who m.8 Dec.1907 Mary Tillott d.1920, he then m.1925 Amy /Annabel Baldwin of Eye b.1904 d.1988

☐

Great grandfather was John Bray Flowerdew b.1836 Corn miller of Wortham, & Elizabeth Green

☐

Great x2 grandfather Thomas Fisher Flowerdew b.1785 d.1853 of Wortham & Eye, & Jane Bray of Diss b.1796 d.1860

☐

Great x3 grandfather John Flowerdew of Wortham d.1833 & Anne Salmon of Wortham d.1837

☐

Great x4 grandfather Thomas Flowerdew c.1716 d.1805 of Redgrave & Garboldisham, & Elizabeth Hagtree b.1721 d.1803 widow of John Fisher of Redgrave

☐

Great x5 grandfather Thomas Flowerdew B.1685 d.1774 of Wortham & Redgrave m.1711 Grace Colman of Bressingham d.1774

☐

Great x6 grandfather Thomas Flowerdew of South Lopham christened 30 May 1649, Eye buried 30 Nov. 1727, m. 12 Oct. 1675 Martha Howchin of Rickinghall Superior d.1711

☐

Great x7 grandfather Nathaniel Flowerdew of Eye, Woollen Draper d.1670 who had property Eye & Mellis, m.16 Jan. 1636 Mary Whiting of Stoke Ash

☐

Possibly Great x8 grandfather thought likely Samuel Flowerdew Curate of Mellis who died in 1681 buried at Eye, though also another Samuel Flowerdew of Eye son of Nathaniel Flowerdew curate of Lopham b.1637

☐

and/or Great x9 grandfather Samuel Flowerdew of Eye (thought born 1575-90) & unknown first wife Anne? 2nd wife? Elizabeth / Martha / Mathy Burrows m. 23 June 1611, Samuel died, his will passed 12 May 1653

☐

Thought son of Martin Flowerdew of Hethersett b.1548, one of John Flowerdew's seven offspring, Thomasine Flowerdew Martin's daughter married Richard of Occold & Harleston

☐ John Flowerdew of Hethersett b.1500 d.1565 (he the cause of the Kett Rebellion) m. Kate / Catherine Sheres of Ashwellthorpe daughter of William Sheres of Ashwellthorpe and Elizabeth daughter of William Forster of Wymondham.

☐ Whose father was William Flowerdew b.1470 d.1536 married to Katherine Hall.

Before his time as noted earlier the records are sparse and the family name is written in several forms, there is much room for research, and indeed it would be interesting to pursue the name back through the French? roots.

From the 'Local' point of view, each and every forefather of mine for the last four hundred years, have come from a village within a ten mile circle, with most from less than half that. And for even more rural cred' all their wives also came from those same villages. Indeed seems I'm the first to go beyond this tiny area for a wife in a half millenium.

On my mother's side we have less information- Pamela Locket was daughter of Alfred Lockett of Dickleburgh and Eva Spooner, of Norwich (Trowse?) daughter of Francis Frances.

Alf was son of village publican, and policeman, Lanky Lockett son of Fiddy Lockett an itinerant fiddle playing wherry-man who settled here having met his wife-to-be at what became the Zoo out by the Moor.

There are also near illegible gravestones of several ancient Flowerdews in Dickleburgh churchyard.

Fictional Flowerdews

As well as inclusion in other's biographies and appearing 'in character' on the radio adaptation of Terry Pratchett's Good Omens other Flowerdews have been embodied as purely literary inventions. There's a Rev'd Flowerdew in Vanity Fair by Thackeray. The character Uncle Rupert Flowerdew, was Ned Seagoon's Uncle, featured in The Goon Show, 105, episode 6, 5th series, where Peter Sellers has a catchphrase "This is madness, do you hear me? Madness!"

Bob's other books

What to do When

-timely notes of monthly tasks in each and every area of the garden,

 "there's a right time for every job- and it was probably last month", very handy for newer gardeners who are taking it all on the first time, and also for us older hands who are not keeping up as well as we did

Grow Your Own Kitchen garden & Pantry
-this is invaluable, not just how to grow but all the ways to then store, preserve & process your crops, an essential guide to becoming your own delicatessen.

Really Help Butterflies
being Volume II of 'Plant Companions and Co-lives' There's little point planting 'flowers to help butterflies' any more than making the North sea bigger to help cod stocks. We need <u>grow those plants their larvae eat</u>. This is an A-Z of wild and garden plants and which of our native butterfly caterpillars THEIR FOLIAGE will sustain.

Really help your plants
Plants and other plants, their good & bad companions and worst weeds'
this being Volume I of 'Plant Companions and Co-lives'
An A-Z of wild and garden plants and recorded effects between these and other plants we need to know about whenever planning or planting our gardens.

Really help your garden ecology
Plants and co-lives; their associated fauna: insects, nematodes, bacteria, fungi large & small and shared

viruses

this being Volume III of 'Plant Companions and Co-lives'

Interactions between our native and garden plants and all the varied forms of life they coexist with and not covered in volumes I & II.

Really help your crops
An edited compilation of all three volumes for the most important interactions, those with our crop plants.

Greenhouse, cloche and tunnel gardening, Growing under cover
What it says on the cover, the distillation of my forty years of experience of protected cropping, including historical development, ways and means, what you need to consider, what you can grow with practical advice on each.

Pulpit in the potting shed
My 'philosophy' expressed in limerick, verse and song.
A penchant to word play

Recycle & Reuse stuff in your garden
My first e-book and best seller, not ever been printed to save paper, exactly what the cover says;

simple garden upcycling uses for all sorts of waste products and junk.
You may use, repeat, copy, distribute by any means any idea from this book with my blessing.

The Companion Garden (Good Companions in USA) (pub. Kyle Cathie)
this my first published book was a delightful little illustrated volume of the benefits mixing plants can offer to us, other creatures and each other. (Several editions all sadly out of print with signed copies of first hardback now quite collectable.)

Bob Flowerdew's Complete Book of Companion Gardening (Kyle Cathie)
here I explore the numerous ways plants interact with other flora and fauna about them, with historical observations, and how we can use these to our advantage. I find it hard to understand why some alleged 'scientists' claim companion planting is base-less. It would be stranger still if with hundreds of thousands of plants and critters in our gardens to find that none interacted in any way other than by being eaten.

The Organic Gardener (Hamlyn-Reed Octopus)
my organic methods in detail including an illustrated plan view of my garden, full of luscious

photos of my flowers and produce taken by Jerry Harpur.
In soft back as **Bob Flowerdew's Organic Garden**. Now sadly out of print though re-worked and re-issued in updated revised forms as **Go Organic**, and **Organic Garden Basics** (Hamlyns).

Bob Flowerdew's Complete Fruit Book (Kyle Cathie)
an encyclopaedic testimonial to the delights fruits and nuts offer to the gardener, the gourmet and to us all.
Full descriptions, instructions and alternative uses, and with my own recipes. Includes not just the usual soft and orchard fruits but also those we can glean from the wild, those unknown edible ornamentals, and those fruits you may come across in a good supermarket or on a foreign holiday. Now out in a carefully revised and expanded edition, and in nearly two dozen foreign languages.
Also combined with Jekka's Complete Herb, and Bigg's Complete Vegetables in a comprehensive edible encyclopaedia of Vegetables, herbs and fruit (Kyle Cathie).

Bob Flowerdew's Organic Bible (Kyle Cathie)
How to be Organic.
Very beautiful photographs (204) in this book all taken in my garden are in themselves lasting

testimonials to the methods, and to the exquisite quality of Organic flowers, fruits and vegetables. All you really need to know.
Now out in a thoroughly revised and updated edition with even more emphasis on encouraging wild life whilst growing your own food and with all new photography.

The No work garden (Kyle Cathie)
in this comic diatribe of vitriol poured enthusiastically on the heads of experts, designers and instant garden makeovers I explain how much of conventional gardening advice is not wrong but is rather inappropriate. I show easier ways of getting more pleasure & production from your garden for much less effort or expense. Good for non-expert gardeners, and older hands will also find much to amuse and inform.
This is THE book you NEED to read BEFORE you start.

The Gourmet Gardener (Kyle Cathie) -
with the emphasis on quality; it's all about taste, flavour, texture, variety and seasonality. This book is not about feeding a family of twelve from an allotment, or just how to produce fodder reliably. It is all about producing really tasty tucker. Growing the very best for yourself!

Going Organic (Kyle Cathie)
this is the greener gardeners guide to solving the pest, disease and cultural problems a gardener will likely encounter along with their most natural cures and preventatives. It's a comprehensive introduction to all those greener and organic methods you can employ to avoid pitfalls and errors, woes and foes and also a reference book for the common pests, diseases and their solutions.

Grow your own, Eat your own (Kyle Cathie)
yet more of my idiosyncratic but very pragmatic approach, this time to storing and preserving your own produce. It is not difficult to grow lots of your own delicious produce but far harder to do so over the whole year. Growing food is only half the story, you also need to harvest, store, process and preserve in a host of different ways to feed your family more fully and happily- so be your own delicatessen, confectioner §and brewer as well as greengrocer and cook.
**** And now available in French!!!****

Bob's Basics (Kyle Cathie)
Six compact volumes covering the most important areas of greener and organic gardening, their titles say it all.
Composting
Companion Planting

Weeding without chemicals
Pruning, Training and Tidying
Simple green Pest and Disease control
Sowing, Planting, Watering and Feeding

Bob also co-authored-
The complete book of vegetables, herbs and fruit - available in many languages and editions (Kyle Cathie)
The complete manual of Organic Gardening (Headline)
Gardeners Question Time All Your Problems Solved (Orion),
Gardeners Question Time Plant Chooser (Kyle Cathie)
Gardeners Question Time Tips & Techniques (Kyle Cathie).

Plus there is much useful information gratis on my website www.bobflowerdew.com and daily notes on what's happening in my garden on Twitter @FlowerdewBob

Printed in Great Britain
by Amazon